Narratives of
Inclusive Teaching

Disability
Studies in
Education

Susan L. Gabel and Scot Danforth
General Editors

Vol. 25

The Disability Studies in Education series is part of the Peter Lang Education list.
Every volume is peer reviewed and meets
the highest quality standards for content and production.

PETER LANG
New York • Bern • Berlin
Brussels • Vienna • Oxford • Warsaw

Srikala Naraian
and Sarah L. Schlessinger

Narratives of
Inclusive Teaching

Stories of *Becoming* in the Field

PETER LANG
New York • Bern • Berlin
Brussels • Vienna • Oxford • Warsaw

Library of Congress Cataloging-in-Publication Data

Names: Naraian, Srikala, author. | Schlessinger, Sarah (Sarah L.), author.
Title: Narratives of inclusive teaching: stories of becoming in the field /
Srikala Naraian, Sarah Schlessinger.
Description: New York: Peter Lang, 2021.
Series: Disability studies in education; Vol. 25 | ISSN 1548-7210
Includes bibliographical references and index.
Identifiers: LCCN 2020052468 (print) | LCCN 2020052469 (ebook) |
ISBN 978-1-4331-8478-9 (paperback) | ISBN 978-1-4331-8479-6 (ebook pdf)
ISBN 978-1-4331-8480-2 (epub) | ISBN 978-1-4331-8481-9 (mobi)
Subjects: LCSH: Inclusive education. | Children with
disabilities—Education. | Children with social disabilities—Education. |
Educational equalization. | Special education teachers.
Classification: LCC LC3965 .N37 2021 (print) | LCC LC3965 (ebook) |
DDC 371.9—dc23
LC record available at https://lccn.loc.gov/2020052468
LC ebook record available at https://lccn.loc.gov/2020052469
DOI 10.3726/b18136

Bibliographic information published by **Die Deutsche Nationalbibliothek**.
Die Deutsche Nationalbibliothek lists this publication in the "Deutsche
Nationalbibliografie"; detailed bibliographic data are available
on the Internet at http://dnb.d-nb.de/.

To
Adam, Harley, Jessica, Molly, Peter, Rena and Taiyo

Contents

Acknowledgments

Many people and places must share in the completion of this book. We are grateful that the institutional location of Teachers College was available as a convenient site to meet with our teacher-graduate-participants whose experiences we have narrated in this book. We appreciated the opportunity to welcome them back into this location where conversations about theory and practice could take new form in light of their recent experiences as certified teachers. Our professional roles (past and present) within the Department of Curriculum and Teaching and in the programs for Inclusive Education provided the opportunity to meet students with shared commitments to social justice for marginalized youth. Most importantly, we owe our heartfelt thanks to Taiyo, Rena, Peter, Molly, Jessica, Harley and Adam, without whose generous interest in our research and willing participation in the study, this book would not have been possible. Their words, emotions, musings, aspirations, and commitments have significantly shifted the ways we think about inclusion and teacher education for inclusion. We have been changed because of them.

As I continue to build and grow my understandings and practices of inclusivity, I, Sarah, am grateful to the many teachers and students that I work with who continue to push me to stretch my theory and practice. My perspective grows through our conversations and shared experiences. I am particularly grateful to Celia Oyler for grounding me in the greater purpose of this work and mentoring me into the worlds of inclusivity and academia. Her mentorship and my membership in the inclusive education community at Teachers College allowed me to make some sense of the inequities in education I had seen as a class-room teacher. Within that community, I am particularly grateful to Srikala Naraian, a mentor, colleague, and a friend who, with unparalleled kindness and patience, continues to help me negotiate my work as a researcher in the field of Disability Studies in Education. I owe much of my understanding of the complexities of inclusive education to these two women. I would also like to thank my family for instilling in me a deep belief in the pursuit of knowledge. To my parents, thank you both for your own commitments to equity and social justice and your willingness to listen to me jabber on about inclusive education. Finally, to my amazing wife, Jamie, who chose to marry me in the midst of my writing anxiety for this book, thank you for partnering me with your perspective, knowledge, thoughtfulness, criticality, strength and unwavering support.

Research and writing is never a solitary endeavor. I, Srikala, am grateful for the numerous ways in which my students continually compel me to clarify my thinking and to seek opportunities alongside them to deepen what we know about inclusive education and how we come to know it. Additionally, I could not sustain my scholarly pursuits without the generous encouragement from colleagues and mentors both within and outside Teachers College, within and outside the US. Their faith in my scholarship has permitted, in significant measure, the risks I have been able to take when delivering some of the insights we have been able to include in this book. As always, I am grateful for the quietly proud support extended by my daughter, Maegha, and for the opportunity to live and work in a city which not only presents visceral challenges to inclusivity everyday but also demands real-time response(s) that must congeal with its aspirations.

We thank the team at Peter Lang Publishing for supporting us in bringing this project to fruition and to Susan Gabel and Scot Danforth, editors of the Disability Studies in Education series, within which this book could find a ready home. Their commitments allows us to continue to pursue our own. Inclusive of Scot and Susan, we extend our gratitude to the Disability Studies in Education community and the platform we collectively create to question the system as it is.

Introduction

Many researchers in the field of disability studies in education, including ourselves, are engaged in teacher education programs that require both coursework and fieldwork (student teaching or practica). Such experiences generally call for ongoing relationships with practicing teachers, negotiation with school partners, encounters with state licensure systems, and familiarity with accountability procedures in schools. Preparing teachers for inclusion is embedded within this assemblage of social activity that has, for us, inevitably come to inform the conceptualization of inclusion itself. Our struggle as researchers and teacher educators has been to reconcile this process with our commitment to the equitable education of students with disabilities[1] that we brought to this work in the first place. This book is our attempt to explore that struggle.

As scholars situated within a disability studies tradition, we are first and foremost unequivocally committed to emancipatory modes of practice that understand disability not as a problem or a deficit within a person, but as emergent within the interactions of individuals with social, cultural, political and legal institutions in society. Our work as teacher educators is grounded in this fundamental commitment to the recognition of disability as a valued form of human variation that requires a vigilant monitoring of the ideology of *ability* which circulates within school systems, categorizing some populations as incompetent or deficient. Teachers, we remind our students and ourselves, must recognize how social, physical and attitudinal barriers produce disability, and should respond actively to mitigate their debilitating effects on individuals, in this case, students in schools. Yet, our experiences over the years with our own students (teacher candidates) as well as our investigations of teacher practices in schools have demanded that we articulate a more complex position. Repeatedly, our students and teacher-participants in our studies have shown us that the work of teaching for inclusion is complex, often contradictory, and sometimes defies the priorities brought by disability studies scholars (Naraian, 2017; Naraian & Schlessinger, 2017). We have found that there are few visible markers of practice that can be unequivocally asserted as necessary for inclusion at all times or everywhere.

This poses particular dilemmas for us as we prepare new teachers for this work. While we now know that teaching for inclusion is a continuous, unfinished process (Booth, 2009), we simultaneously assert that there is much about becoming an inclusive educator that remains unknown. For instance, in what ways does a critical awareness of the ableist, racist, gendered and classist underpinnings of a school system come to inform the professional growth and development of an educator? How do teacher candidates draw on the idealized vision of schooling for equity and social justice to make decisions about what they will teach, to whom, how, and when? These questions are necessary not only to prepare candidates most effectively for this work, but also to continually monitor how we ourselves, as teacher educators, conceptualize inclusion. Our focus, in this book, therefore, is to document a segment of this process of becoming an inclusive educator, namely, the early stages of entry into the field. The question we have taken up in this book is: How do novice teachers prepared in higher education settings for inclusive practices begin to construct their professional identities within the context of their schools? We hope that this will ultimately deepen our understandings of inclusion and inclusive practice and our preparation and support of novice teachers.

(Re)storying Teachers, Recognizing Agency

The premise of this book, then, is that the stories that teachers tell are important both to understand the phenomenon of inclusion, as well as to conceptualize how teachers come to understand themselves. We expect that teachers' sense-making efforts will give us deeper clues into the meanings of inclusion within schools. We simultaneously recognize such sense-making to be grounded in the material contexts of practice, indeed as inseparable from them. In that regard, we do not categorize these teachers as heroic, passive, compliant or negligent. Instead, we understand teachers' agency for inclusion to be *situated* and as emergent from the interplay of biographical and material-discursive contextual elements that collectively create the conditions within which inclusive practice is enacted (Danforth & Naraian, 2015). As we navigate through different intellectual traditions (described later in this chapter) we find ourselves continually refining and demystifying such *situatedness*. We have gradually come to understand that our efforts to do so both preserve and challenge the centrality of the teacher figure in this phenomenon. While this has provoked some unease, it has also stimulated us to adopt a "jumping and straddling" of epistemological positions (Ellingson, 2011). We will explain this further in subsequent pages. But first, we begin with our primary commitment to teacher stories.

The Significance of Teachers' Stories

Teachers typically bring a continual, unending stream of stories to share about their students, their interactions with colleagues, with families and with community members. They share stories about curriculum-making and the texts that affect their students and their classroom communities. They overflow with stories about students' interactions with each other, with texts and with other adults in the community. They are filled with stories about administrative and bureaucratic decisions that produce success or failure for their students and for themselves. Listening to teachers, we come to understand the beliefs and assumptions that animate their work, the struggles they uphold, the conditions they find supportive, the vulnerabilities they bear, and the successes and constraints they experience. "Exploring this multifaceted knowledge more fully through attention to the way that teachers' stories are told, their language and imagery, their drama or repetitiveness, one can disclose the underlying conceptualizations and reconceptualizations of the educational situation and come to a better understanding of how teachers do their work and why" (Elbaz-Luwisch, 2005, p. ix). Understanding how and why teachers take up inclusive practices, we additionally argue, can help us refine our understandings of inclusion itself.

The privileging of stories itself is premised on distinguishing between multiple modes of thinking. Narrative researchers Clandinin and Connelly (2000) describe a distinction between thinking narratively and thinking formalistically. Thinking narratively about the experiences of individuals and communities is to understand events as continuous with other experiences across time; to recognize people as engaged in a process of change; to perceive the meanings of action not as self-evident but as expression of other narrative histories; to remain cognizant that interpretations of actions/events are always subject to change, and are necessarily characterized by tentativeness rather than certainty; and, to recognize the centrality of context in interpreting people's lives and the inevitable situatedness of actions and intentional states that are not readily predictable (Clandinin & Connelly, 2000; Stone-Mediatore, 2000). The formalistic approach, on the other hand, relies on the frameworks we bring to assess what things are and how they can be different. Conversely, "it is a view that things are never what they are but are rather what our framework or points of view or perspective or outlook makes of them" (Clandinin & Connelly, 2000, p. 39). Inevitably, for inclusive education researchers, these forms of thinking produce sites of significant tension. When we observe teachers engage in practice that, from a critical disability studies lens, suggests ableist norms, we are likely to interpret such teaching as problematic and as defeating the aims of inclusion. Narrative thinking, however, requires that we remain open to the possibility of other interpretations; we are called to monitor our own narrative histories when working at the site of these tensions.

Narrative knowing begins with the stories that are told by people. In doing thus, it upholds individual agency as significant for understanding experience. Some scholars argue that representations of experience that portray the subject as the primary agent are misleading because they obscure the discursive context that make available particular forms of actions and thought. Experience, they argue, cannot exist outside the discourses used to represent it (Scott, 2014). Others, however, have noted the power of narratives to disclose the historical-material conditions within which experiences are formed as well as the potential for alternative ways of being/thinking implicit within stories that may be unavailable in larger, widely circulating stories (Moya, 2000; Stone-Mediatore, 2000). We orient towards the latter position; in privileging experience via narrative, we recognize the narrative experience as epistemically significant for generating important theoretical knowledge.

A narrative mode of inquiry does not presume that the stories people tell about their experiences are their own, though they do not simply make them up (Frank, 2010). Rather, stories are important not only for the construction of selves, but also in "making life social" (p.15). They perform important functions in guiding individuals to interpret experiences and to act in particular ways within social environments. In that regard, they are crucial for teachers' ongoing identity work (Elbaz-Luwisch, 2005). If the primary work of stories is to make the earth habitable, then they simultaneously also teach people to understand who they are (Frank, 2010). Yet, the self that becomes articulated through these stories is not necessarily a stable, unitary self. On the contrary, stories shared by individuals are always partial, registering a particular constellation of social actors and events that are made visible and relevant at particular moments in time and which do not follow a linear progression. To surface these constellations more strongly in this book, we have, in many instances, emphasized the collectivities within which the teachers in this book found themselves. Doing this inevitably

de-centered teacher agency, bumping up uneasily against our fundamentally narrative stance. Still, we found we could illustrate agency as
an embodied, rather than a purely cerebral phenomenon when we paid
greater attention to bodily attachments (Feely, 2016). In other words,
teachers' affective capacities and performances were important for our
understanding of inclusive practice (Naraian & Khoja-Moolji, 2016).

Teachers, like the rest of us, enact multiple versions of themselves—
in different places at different times, with different social partners. In
that regard, while we are constrained by our data to pay particular
attention to the period when the teachers in this book were just setting
out to become teachers, we expect that their own written reflections five
years later will illustrate the ways in which the work of storying actors
moves through time in non-linear ways, capturing the multiplicity of
selves that populate one's experiences. Collectively, the narratives we
present offer a provocative, albeit partial, window into the ongoing process of "becoming" teachers.

Preparing to Understand Teacher Agency

Inasmuch as a narrative accounting of teachers as always already agentive is an important place to begin our work in understanding the journey of teachers, it may also be helpful to review how teacher agency
has been traditionally investigated, and the assumptions within those
approaches. Within inclusive education scholarship premised on disability studies in education, teachers are generally presumed to be
agentive when they are able to recognize the deficit-based practices
within schools, and work to disrupt them in ways that can benefit
marginalized students, with a particular focus on students with disabilities. They are, in short, charged with being agents of change who
can, within their own realms of experience work to dismantle ableist
and exclusionary structures (Ashby, 2012; Oyler, 2011). Important as
this trope may be for the development of liberatory practices that can
benefit students with disabilities, it also assumes agency to be a stable, internal property that can be transported across contexts. Such a
position, however, is contrary to a narrative approach described above,
wherein experience remains bound to the places, people, events, and

ideas that circulate within stories. Some scholars have offered ways of understanding teacher agency that support the premises of this book.

Priestly, Biesta, and Robinson (2015) offer an ecological model to understand teacher agency as a form of achievement. Encompassing three dimensions—the *iterational* (relating to life-histories and professional biographies), the *practical-evaluative* (enactment within concrete structural, cultural and material conditions) and the *projective* (referencing short-term and long-term futures)—this model suggests that teacher agency is always informed by past experiences, orientated in some way or the other towards the future and enacted in a particular situation that is subject to a set of affordances and constraints. This ecological model radically shifts conceptions of teacher agency away from individual bodies/minds to include a more expansive consideration of a wide range of influences that inform teacher enactment. Teachers, these authors suggest, can be said to *achieve* agency when they are able to choose between different options that are made available to them in different situations. They also caution against using notions of teacher capacity to understand teacher agency; while the former may be necessary, it is not sufficient.

The model offered by Priestly, Biesta, and Robinson (2015) bears some linkage to an understanding of teacher agency as always socio-culturally mediated (Vygotsky, 1986). In other words, teachers' exercise of agency does not emanate solely from within the individual but is in fact inseparable from the school structures and the particular cultural resources made available to them, including the policies and mandates of the school, norms of teacher professionalism and student achievement, their beliefs and commitments, and the larger sociopolitical context in which they carry out their work (Pantic, 2015; Priestly et al., 2015). Drawing collectively on the benefits of these approaches, we take up a situated notion of agency that is located within the cultural worlds in which it emerges, but which is not pre-determined by the discourses prevalent within them (Holland, Lachiotte, Skinner, & Cain, 1998).

The above frameworks for understanding agency are generative for us in two important ways: firstly, they allow us to retain our narrative approach to teachers that privileges the stories they tell about their experiences as inclusive educators; secondly, they simultaneously permit us to remain deeply cognizant of the nature of the conditions within which teachers must enact inclusion. Collectively, they allow us to retain the commitments to students with disabilities and their families that animates our scholarly commitments, while continually remaining mindful of the complexity of teacher enactments of socially just pedagogy. It is this complexity in which both teachers and researchers are entangled, that draws us continually towards notions of agency that can "extend beyond the skin" of the individual (Puar, 2017). It is not surprising then that, we feel simultaneously compelled to pursue theorists who argue that agency is distributed across human and non-human actors (Barad, 2007, 2008; DeLanda, 2006). Still, we uphold the capacity of bodies to affect and be affected by others as an important element within such mixed collectivities (Ahmed, 2006; DeLanda, 2006; Postma, 2016. We therefore hold in some productive tension competing views of agency and competing ways of knowing; we are motivated by the hope that doing so can offer us important insights into how the becoming of novice teachers can be enabled/constrained.

Our Theoretical Attachments: Disability Studies in Education with a Critical Realism

As scholars who inhabit different locations within different (albeit intersecting) professional trajectories, we bring a range of theoretical commitments that collectively help us to set the stage for this book. For Kala, the search for a complex understanding of teacher work produced a scholarly journey that, while always rooted in the commitments of a disability studies in education, has entailed an exploration of multiple traditions including sociocultural anthropology, transnational feminisms, postpositivist realism, spatial theory and more recently, posthumanism. For Sarah, the investment in the education of forgotten or pushed-out students led to a belief in teacher capacity and a scholarly journey rooted in disability studies in education, critical race theory, and affect theory.

The following description reflects our collective engagement with these bodies of work in the context of our shared commitment to understanding and improving inclusive practices in schools. For both of us, the place we begin is disability studies in education. For disability studies scholars, disablement is understood as produced through externally imposed barriers that oppress individuals with disabilities and prevent their access to, and inclusion within, all walks of life (Ware, 2010). Disability studies in education (DSE), shines a specific spotlight on the ways in which this disablement is enacted and reified through the practices of schooling for many groups and individuals (Danforth & Gabel, 2006; Gabel, 2005). Over the last decade, DSE scholars have produced a sophisticated critique of the epistemological foundations of schooling that delegitimize disability and disclosed the many ways in which schooling systems sort and categorize students to produce labels of incompetence and failure. Increasingly, scholars in this field have deepened such analyses to account for the ways in which different social identifiers such as race/ethnicity, class, gender, immigrant status, among others, intersect with disability (Connor, Ferri, & Annama, 2016). Steadily eschewing medicalized, individualized, deficit-oriented understandings of disability, such analyses have instead disclosed the complex workings of social and institutional structures that produce oppressive experiences for students and their families.

Critical race theory (CRT) similarly understands race as societally produced and calls for an interrogation of societal systems and structures that privilege Whiteness (Delgado & Stefancic, 2017). The scholars of CRT in education invite the use of storytelling to disrupt dominant narratives of schooling by foregrounding the narratives of those "who have experienced victimization by racism and ableism firsthand," (Watts & Erevelles, 2004, p. 274). Even as these theoretical traditions have been collectively deployed to disrupt normative discourses of "Whiteness," "Smartness," and "Goodness" (Leonardo & Broderick, 2011), for the large part, they have remained relatively separate. This might be owed to their complicated histories of oppression; for instance, the use of disability to justify the subjugation of people of color (Watts & Erevelles, 2004). This intersection of "justified" discrimination, segregation, and oppression is a ripe ground for exploring the complex workings of systems of exclusion (Annamma, Connor, & Ferri, 2013; Watts & Erevelles, 2004). It also serves as a robust resource for various anti-oppressive tools forwarded by each scholarly community.

These intersectional approaches offer new directions to under-standing disability and difference. Looking retrospectively at the theo-retical web that we have constructed over time, we begin this study of teachers from a more *critical realist* position (Maxwell, 2012). A critical realism is suspicious of a constructivism that is rooted in a material-discursive binary and which privileges language in the construction of experience. We are aware that the term *realism* instinctively arouses the concern of constructivists, including DSE scholars and some narrative inquirers, since it seems to imply that there is one correct description of that reality, or one "truth." However, unlike the naive realism associ-ated with positivism, *critical realism* acknowledges mental states, inten-tions, and concepts, as part of the real world that affords us a unique perspective or standpoint on reality. In other words, reality is socially constructed, but *not only* socially constructed (Moya, 2000). For criti-cal realists, the intertwining of material embodiment with mental con-structs in the constitution of experience creates room for both error and accuracy within our interpretations of our experiences that over time may be revised. It assumes that there are causally significant features in the world (e.g., racism, sexism, ableism, etc.) that account for systems of exploitation and which create politically salient social categories (Mohanty, 2000). For instance, disability studies scholar Tobin Siebers (2008) has argued that the ideology of ability that pervades the "built environment," in society serves as a causally significant feature that marks the embodied experiences of people with disabilities in discrim-inatory ways.

A realist position argues that the consequences of one's social location exert particular constraints on our judgements and analysis (Hau, 2000). Such interpretations of experience may not simply reflect a naive appropriation of cultural stories but could actually have trans-formative effects. Third World feminist Chandra Mohanty takes up the affordance of this material-discursive nature of experience to argue for the significance of local narratives that can, through a historical-materialist lens produce important insights about marginalized expe-riences (Mohanty, 2003). In her exploration of the labor of Third World women, she acknowledges that these women's understanding of expe-riences appeared to have appropriated capitalist ideologies, even as it had brought material improvement in their lives. Still, the types of agency that surfaced in their narratives could only be made visible by restorying their experience that could then counter essentialist under-standings of Third World women produced through "western eyes" (Mohanty, 2003).

The importance attached to the subjective interpretation of expe-rience, despite the possibility of error, attests to the fluid nature of any category, including disability, and the continual "becoming" implicit within its appropriation (Erevelles, 2011). A critical realist position emphasizes the "multiplicity" of one's experience; the effects of one's multiple social locations weave continually and unevenly through space and time to constitute one's experience. Disability, then may be experienced in ways that are contingent on this "multi-locationality" (Brah, 2003) of persons along various dimensions of class, race, gen-der, etc. Said differently, meanings of disability are never self-evident. The significance of this for understanding teachers and schools lies in the contingent nature of inclusive enactments and the imperative to allow for the possibility of change within them. This also means that the practices of educators who claim an inclusive orientation, will, by necessity, look different in various sociocultural contexts. Additionally, for teacher educators, like ourselves, it not only calls for us to prepare teachers for uncertain outcomes but also for us to embrace such ambi-guity as a salient feature of teacher preparation for inclusivity.

As is evident, it is the recognition of the material-discursive nature of experience, or its "complex embodiment," (Siebers, 2008), that has remained a continual thread in our efforts to straddle the competing commitments to students with disabilities and to educators charged with teaching for inclusion. In continuing to recognize the affordances of realism, the "agential realism" of Karen Barad, associated with *new materialist* scholarship, suggests other ways of understanding agency in schools. Specifically, Barad's theory incorporates material and dis-cursive, human and non-human and natural and cultural actors in the description of a phenomena to de-center the individual as the sole originator of agentic enactment. Human agency in this framing, is not the property of the individual, but one of many entangled agencies that produce the phenomena through intra-action. Unlike the critical realist position advanced by Maxwell (2012), for Barad, ontology (how something comes to be) and epistemology (how we come to know) are not separate, but mutually constituted. She seeks an *onto-epistemology*, where *knowing is in being* (2008). The process of coming to know agents-within-phenomena implicates not only how we come to know, but also the fact that *how* we come to know brings into being *what* we come to know.

This orientation of new materialist[2] scholarship has implications for how we recognize (in)equity within schools. For instance, scholars in disability studies in education have questioned the epistemological foundations of special educational systems that are premised on notions of disability defined by non-disabled priorities and experiences. They have assumed an ontological stance that understands disability as fundamentally socially constructed. Even as these challenges have been critical for understandings of disability in schools that depart from traditional deficit-laden perspectives, new materialisms pose a challenge to these assumptions in requiring us to take up an *onto-epistemological* position. In invoking multiple human and non-human agencies, it compels consideration of how matter and meaning (the material and discursive) are mutually constituted.

The turn to reinvigorating materiality in our analyses simultaneously requires attending to the circulation of affects and teachers' own affective attachments. Embodied and emotive reactions to the material and the discursive move individuals towards and away from objects and actions of pleasure and pain. As Ahmed (2010) explains, we become attached to objects or ideas through their affective projections. Objects and ideas gain meaning through our desires for happiness and its pursuit or avoidance, or through the fear of shame as well as its capacity to humble and humanize us. Happiness is anticipated from, for example, receiving praise or achieving success, while shame is often derived from feelings of fear, failure, and being an imposter (Probyn, 2010). These attachments as experienced through the body work to constitute meaning and direct movement of people and objects. The affective performances in the production of inclusive classrooms has not received significant attention in the literature on preparing teachers for inclusive pedagogy.

Barad's post-humanist stance as well as affect theories, may on first glance, work against the humanist approach to teachers that we have begun to articulate in this chapter. After all, we have committed to privilege the agency of teachers in the narration of their experiences. How can a narrative approach be reconciled with post-humanist frameworks that encompass human and non-human entities (Braidotti, 2018)? How can we attend to human agency if the unit of analysis is the phenomenon rather than the individual (Barad, 2007)? These are important dilemmas and we do not claim to have resolved them. Our efforts to navigate them, however, are themselves characteristic of the open-endedness of these approaches. The "diffractive" methodology that Barad proposes does not eliminate the significance of an interpretive approach that relies on storying teachers' experiences. It requires that different texts and theories be read intra-actively through one another. It also compels us to recognize that even when we take an interpretive approach to teachers, we are obligated to implicate ourselves as researchers, that is, our theories, our experiences, our sociopolitical locations, as intra-acting with other agencies to produce the phenomenon of inclusion (Barad, 2007; Clandinin, 2013).

The significance of bringing together these different forms of knowing is that they allow us to explore multiple ways to accomplish the goal of storying the professional lives of new teachers. Collectively, our theoretical attachments afforded us the means to undertake nuanced descriptions of teacher practice that can reflect the complex nature of inclusive pedagogy.

Our Struggles

Even as we feel intellectually prepared to undertake the project of describing the work of novice teachers institutionally prepared to teach for inclusion, these frames simultaneously require that we, as researchers, engage in particular social and intellectual struggles. This work cannot be accomplished without such struggles and will undoubtedly surface in the descriptions of the teachers in the book. We categorize them in the following ways.

The Threat to Our Commitments to Equity

As we acknowledged earlier, we straddle competing commitments, that is, to students with disabilities and their families as well as teachers in schools. While we remain mindful of the experiences that characterize the location of each of these groups within school systems, our efforts to understand teacher practice necessarily requires that we sometimes bracket our recognition of the ways in which disability is performed in schools. Such bracketing allows us to extend an asset-based focus on teachers as learners who require particular kinds of supports. This process also means that we are less able to take an overtly ideological stance in a way that unequivocally denounces the less-than-equitable practices in school. As we navigate through multiple ideological positions, we wonder—has our commitment to students with disabilities been diluted? How can we re-assert ourselves as advocates for students who have historically been dehumanized by ableist school systems, while we recognize the conditions within which teachers enact their own commitments to inclusion?

Scholarly Identities

The struggle to categorically align ourselves with one position rather than another has also complicated our own scholarly identities. If the intellectual tradition which we see as our scholarly "home," that is, disability studies in education, calls for a clear and unequivocal critique of schooling systems and practices that are premised on ableist norms, can we truly characterize ourselves as "doing" disability studies? Much of our work has privileged the (re)articulation of teachers' stories rather than a focus on the oppressive features of schooling even as we are deeply aware of the latter. Does an engagement with special education discourse, structure and practice automatically disqualify us from claiming to be scholars in the field of disability studies? Or, are we critical special education scholars? How does that matter, and to whom?

In contemplating these identity dilemmas, we have taken courage from the work of Third World feminists who have spoken about the illusory nature of "home" or its continually shifting nature that disallows any certainty about one's location, in this case our location as DSE scholars (Minh-Ha, 2011). We are strengthened by Anzaldúa's notion of a *mestiza* consciousness (Anzaldúa, 1987) that understands that we must be "on both shores at once" in our struggles for equitable practice. The borderlands we inhabit as scholars engaging in this work are no different from the myriad borderlands that our own students, teacher candidates, and teachers encounter when they engage with the material conditions of inclusive practice. We recognize that ambiguity will necessarily characterize this journey we have undertaken. Admittedly, we struggle to always see this as empowering …

Struggles Produced Via Our Own "Multi-locationality"

These scholarly borderlands are even more complicated by our own identity work as we experience our life-narratives contextualized by the same structures and ideologies that we research. For example, for Sarah, experiencing the world as an able-bodied, white, queer, cisgender woman, from an upper-middle-class Jewish family, means a constant navigation of her own intersectional identities and the ways in which she experiences both privilege and oppression. It means continually considering the ways in which her own experiences inform her sense-making of other people's experiences and recognizing the "epistemological racism" and ableism embedded in educational research (Roegman, 2018). What does it mean to be a White woman or an able-bodied woman researching systems that have historically excluded people of color and people with disabilities? How is that further complicated by focusing on other peoples' stories?

For Kala, an able-bodied, straight, cisgendered immigrant female of Asian (Indian) origin, reflections on diversity and equity are inseparable from the vastly different sociocultural contexts in which she has come to know herself. In other words, like Sarah, inequities of opportunity have assumed multiple forms and locations that do not in any self-evident way suggest privilege or oppression across any social identifier such as race, class, gender, ability, immigrant status, etc. She recognizes that even the title of "faculty of color" that she is assigned within the United States does not necessarily afford her the epistemic standpoint that other faculty of color, particularly African-American faculty, may claim. Perhaps the most significant identifier that has afforded her a unique lens to understanding disability and teacher preparation has been her claim to experiences that are more typical of Third World women and which has come to inform her personal and professional decision-making. In that regard, she struggles with taking up a race-consciousness that can bear fidelity to her life experiences while simultaneously understand its relations with other racialized histories in the United States.

The Context for This Book

In describing our own struggles and attachments that we bring as authors of this book, we do not seek to minimize the contributions of the teachers who have participated in the writing of this book. To the extent their authorial voices are necessary to produce, at this moment in time, the partial stories that we share about their becoming, they are key contributors to this book. We do not draw on their voices merely to "triangulate" what we have found in the data we have collected. We perceive their authorial presence as doing more than simply refuting or concurring with our statements. Instead, we offered our stories *about* them *to* them, in the hope that they would serve as a springboard for their own reflections on their process of becoming. In that regard, our goal is not to collapse our perspectives with theirs, or vice versa. Rather, it is to uphold the kind of reflective community that has typically characterized our relationships. We recognize that there are many other ways to accomplish this goal; still, each of the stories shared in this book offered an opportunity to learn about ourselves collectively, as teachers and teacher educators.

Teacher Candidates/Novice Teachers

The origins of this book lie in our experiences as instructors of a cohort of students enrolled in a secondary inclusive education residency program. This cohort displayed an immediate and deep commitment to the counter-hegemonic praxis of inclusive education. They eagerly took up the ideas, constructs and perspectives we offered from a disability studies lens and sought to fold them into the goals for socially just pedagogy that they brought to their program of study. As part of a larger federally funded teacher residency program, they were embedded in schools throughout their preparatory period while simultaneously taking courses in the evening at the university. Even though we were not directly responsible for the administration of the program, they enrolled in four courses with us where we were the primary instructors. Despite what we perceived as their superior commitment to inclusion in their coursework with us, when they were required to perform their knowledge of teaching students with disabilities on the state certification performance test, all but one failed. Admittedly, the assessment for special education certification is premised on medical model notions of disability, while the coursework for our DSE driven inclusive education program is largely premised on a social model of disability and the disruption of a medical model.

Our initial impetus to investigate the experiences of this cohort, therefore, was to better understand the relevance of our own practice as teacher educators. We wondered if our students might be taking up inclusive education in ways that were perhaps too contrarian or dismissive to function within the reality of exclusionary schooling contexts. Even as we began to look for traces of their sense-making in their curricular projects (Naraian & Schlessinger, 2017) we invited them to participate in a study with us during their first year of teaching. The overwhelmingly affirmative response to our invitation confirmed for us that these teacher-participants valued the space for collaborative reflection with their peers. Additionally, by this time, they had congealed as a group in a way that allowed for animated yet respectful conversations where individuals expressed empathy for each other even as they might disagree with their positions. As their former instructors, we were simply awed by their commitment to collaborative reflective inquiry without any formal preparation for the same. We set out to design the study in ways that could benefit them as budding teachers as well as allow us a rich window into the process of their becoming.

Research Design

It was late summer of 2014, when we invited this cohort of seven newly minted teachers who had been enrolled in the program at the same time (May 2013—August 2014) to participate in our study. On completion of program requirements, all procured employment as educators (with the exception of Adam, all assumed the role of special educators) in the local urban school system. The cohort comprised 4 women (Molly, Jessica, Rena and Harley) and 3 men (Adam, Taiyo and Peter), four of whom were white and three of Asian origin. The group included a former school paraprofessional, a community activist, an artist advocate, former AmeriCorps City Year corps members,[3] and a student fresh from undergraduate studies. Their age ranged from early 20s to early 40s; Peter was the only parent in the group with young children in school at the time of the study.

We organized six meetings for the group during the 2014–2015 academic year. Meetings were held approximately four to six weeks apart, beginning in October 2014 and ending in June 2015. Each meeting followed a simple format—we posed one or two key questions; each person was given an opportunity to reflect and respond. We probed them further whenever necessary. Participants might also question each other during this process. The discussion at each meeting centered on two or three key questions or prompts that we had prepared based on the discussions from earlier meetings (and from separate interviews, discussed below). For example, in the third group session, we asked participants to discuss the idea of competence, what it meant to them and how they experienced that in their work. In at least three of the meetings we engaged them in creating/analyzing graphical representations of some of the ideas that surfaced during these meetings. They used this method to examine the big ideas from the program that surfaced as (ir)relevant during their everyday practice. Each of the meetings took place on the university premises. Except for two meetings, all meetings were attended by all teachers.

During the course of the same year, we also conducted two interviews with each teacher, once during the Fall of 2014 and the other during the Spring of 2015. We either visited them at their schools or met at a local restaurant for these interviews. The purpose of these conversations was to deepen our understandings of their experiences and to probe more deeply on the events and ideas that they shared during the collective meetings.

Collectively, the data we gathered from course-related assignments during their pre-service year, and the collaborative meetings and separate interviews during their first year of teaching offered us an opportunity to imagine the evolution of their professional identities—turning slowly in a three dimensional space as they shifted their experiential focus from university to school, began to engage with the social world of schooling, and encountered the material realities of New York City schools (Clandinin & Connelly, 2000). The stories they shared disclosed how each participated in this process, the resources they brought to it, and how both were constructing this first year experience for them. *Our* stories of them seek to capture the complexity of this process while always leaving it open-ended to further evolve in ways we could not predict. The teachers' stories in this book present another three-dimensional slice of that process, as it were, affording us another means to deepen our understanding of how teachers come to understand inclusion.

Special Education Reform in New York City Schools

The sociopolitical educational context of inclusive teaching plays a significant role in shaping the experiences and stories of these novice teachers. Having graduated from a teacher education program in inclusive education based in New York City, these seven educators all went on to teach in New York City Schools that were in the midst of ongoing special education reform work. In the fall of 2005, in response to the updated legislation of IDEA in 2004, the New York City Department of Education commissioned a citywide analysis of its special education system and the services being provided to the over 1 million students in (at that time) 1,600 public schools in the largest school district in the United States. The Comprehensive Management Review and Evaluation of Special Education Report (Hehir, et al., 2005), commonly referred to as the Hehir Report, uncovered that a "medical model" of disability was guiding the provision of special education services and that consequently the focus of these services was student placement rather than supporting the learning strengths and needs of students. What is more, the placement of individual students was largely premised on the availability of "seats" in special education programs in individual schools rather than by the neighborhood community of the student and, again, the specific strengths and needs of the student.

In response to this comprehensive report, the New York City Department of Education began a new wave of special education reform for the city in 2010. This reform initiative called for New York City Public Schools to close the achievement gap between students with disabilities and their peers without disabilities; provide increased access to, and participation in, the general education curriculum; and create the flexibility to meet the diverse needs of students with disabilities (Citywide Council on Special Education, n.d.). Various actions were taken in pursuit of these goals. New funding formulas were written that incentivized schools to provide more diverse special education programming that would support students with disabilities in integrated co-teaching classrooms.[4] With more schools offering more programming options to provide services to students with disabilities, the Department of Education also determined that they would fund professional development opportunities for educators in schools that undertook specific reforms to provide students with disabilities greater access to the general curriculum. As of the 2012–2013 school year, 18.1% of all NYC students were labeled as special education students with 50.2% of these students receiving special education services in integrated co-teaching classrooms or push-in services in general education classrooms in neighborhood schools. The teachers in this book worked primarily as special educators in these integrated co-teaching classrooms, although some also taught in segregated self-contained classrooms for portions of their day and one only taught in a general education classroom. These ongoing reform efforts and concerns over "seats" and placements continue to be controversial in NYC schools, setting the backdrop for configuring what it meant to be an inclusive educator for the teachers in this book.

Organization of This Book

In the chapters that follow, we take up the narratives of each of the teachers who participated in this study. In each chapter, we first present our research story of their professional lives based on the data we collected. This is followed by a reflection from the teacher that looks retrospectively at the first four years of their teaching careers. This reflection may/may not directly address the themes/ideas from the research narrative. Our decision to place the teachers' stories after our research narrative was made to reflect the particular research methodology we adopted. We did not undertake a collaborative research methodology that engaged the teachers in every aspect of design. This remained an investigation that was driven by our priorities as researchers. We recognize, therefore, the power differential that existed between our participants and us. So, even as we value the mutually respectful relationships we have come to share, we seek to take responsibility for the study with the expectation that its findings are enriched by the reflections of our participants.

In Chapter One, Taiyo's commitments to social justice and the centrality of race and culture in his analysis of his school context moved us towards CRT to frame our exploration of his first year of teaching. Centering his meaning making and experience as a teacher of color, this narrative situates him in a schooling context comprising a predominantly White teaching staff largely unprepared to embrace students with disabilities. The strong connections he experienced with his students were paralleled by his outsider location both as a special educator and a person of color within the community of educators at his school. His practice, struggle, and growth lay in the ways he needed to variously position himself in relation to his students and his co-workers. The chapter surfaces the necessity for relational work with both students and colleagues in the pursuit of inclusive teaching.

In Chapter Two we draw on affect theory to frame Molly's story, one that is characterized by her commitment to doing what is best for all of her students, her responsibility to provide the "right" and "best" services to her students with labeled disabilities, and her anxiety and uncertainty about what any of that work actually looks like. We show

how Molly's inclusive commitment attached itself to objects and people (her students and colleagues) evoking a persistent anxiety that prompted particular trajectories of thought and action. Molly's struggles surface the question of what counts as a service and what may be a *dis*service. In this first year of teaching, Molly's relationship with the DSE-informed foundations of her pedagogy evoked a tension within in her about whose knowledge she should prioritize and whether she had a right to make those decisions. It provoked anxiety about her role as an advocate and educator. Speaking from within a model of inclusion in practice that clearly demarcated students "with" and "without" disabilities, Molly's story interrogates meanings of ability/disability in the classroom.

In Chapter Three, we take up a "diffractive" methodology (Barad, 2007) to examine Peter's experiences. After an initial *interpretive* approach that privileges Peter as a human agent, we read into and through that narrative to understand how he intra-acted with a range of human and cultural "agents" to produce varied meanings of inclusive teaching. Such a "diffractive" reading required us to explore the "storying" of Peter differently. Instead of asking "who is this person," we asked instead: How was Peter constituted as an educator in the intra-activity between various entities that constituted the phenomenon of inclusion in his school? How, when, and with what intensities did Peter intra-act with the other entities implicated within the phenomenon of inclusion? What enactments of inclusion emerged in such intra-action? These questions in conjunction with a narrative approach disclosed Peter's inclusive *teacher-ness* as emerging within his intra-activity with school norms to produce new understandings of teacher competence.

Chapter Four takes a step back from the critical framing of inclusivity to explore personal growth as both new teacher *and* critical special educator in producing the phenomenon of inclusion. It describes Harley's experience of being a young, female, novice, special educator finding her voice in co-teaching relationships with older, male, experienced, general educators. The chapter acknowledges a widely reported phenomenon in co-teaching relationships, that is, the second-class citizenship of special educators. It simultaneously affords an intriguing window into Harley's own processing of this experience vis-a-vis her gender, age, and professional experience. The chapter invites us to consider how multiple ongoing and overlapping "scripts" (Ahmed, 2010) of the right or good way to be in the world inform the development of inclusive teacher identities and the production of inclusion.

Chapter Five is a return to a "diffractive" methodology (Barad, 2007), this time with Jessica as first the human agent and then one of many intra-acting agents. We take up a divergent reading of her experiences to assemble a range of material and discursive, human and non-human actors including school discourses of failure, co-teaching relationships, curricular practices and state-sponsored examinations, that produced inclusion in her context. The material-discursive context in which Jessica was required to display her inclusive *teacher-ness* was constituted through an apparatus of knowing premised on particular understandings of inclusion, teaching, and learning. Going beyond Jessica's skin, as it were, to understand how she is produced by, and within, the intra-action of various agents, this chapter prioritizes the entanglements of inclusive practice to derive a material-discursive conceptualization of both inclusion and teacher agency for inclusion.

Using Annamma & Morrison's (2018) tenets for a DisCrit ecology of a classroom as a framework, Chapter Six focuses on Adam's attempts at and frustrations with working as an activist and an agent for change. The chapter highlights his curricular exploration of the multiple and intersectional markers of difference that have constituted historical and contemporary exclusion in schooling. Through analysis intended to "uncover the relationship between agency, structure, and critique," (Malagon, Huber, & Velez, 2009, p.267) Adam's story engages the complex intersectionality of race and disability, while disclosing his struggle to reframe his thinking to consider his omission of an anti-ableist stance. Ultimately, the chapter surfaces the power positioning of teachers (special and general) and the significance of the specific school context for the enactment inclusion.

In Chapter Seven we draw on both affect theory and a theory of assemblage to help understand the absurdities that constituted the context within which Rena enacted her commitments. We draw on Rena's laughter that accompanied her descriptions of her experiences to unravel the conditions of schooling over which she had little control.

It served as a conduit for the *pedagogical interruptions* she initiated that could alter the affective dimensions of the teaching-learning context. Rena's descriptions of her enactments disclose inclusivity as a material-discursive assemblage of elements, which included an administration soaked with volatility as well as progressive ambitions for students with disabilities in the building; co-teaching structures and relationships that both marked her own sense of incompetence as well as produced an orientation to them (co-teachers) as learners; and, students who pulled her towards them, compelling her determination to orient them to school in positive ways.

In the final chapter, we reflect on the journeys taken by the teachers described in the book and our own in making sense of their stories. We explore the significance of recognizing the complex material-discursive environments in which these teachers were required to develop their competencies as inclusive educators. We argue for teacher capacity for inclusion as lying at the interface of the personal and social. We emphasize the significance of understanding the relations between general, special and inclusive education to delineate teacher competency. We renew the argument for exploring the affective dimension of inclusive practice. Collectively, we call for inclusion to be recognized not as an abstract concept but as a material-discursive arrangement of people, practices and ideas that remains fluid and open-ended.

Notes

1 We acknowledge that many positions may be adopted when selecting language to describe disability as an identifier. Briefly, some use "disabled" to celebrate disability as an identity category, while others have emphasized the assertion of person-first terminology as in "students with disabilities." We support both positions and have ourselves used both these terms in our work. In this book, we have retained person-first terminology, in part to speak alongside our participants.

2 We recognize that many scholars have challenged the "new" in new materialisms; however, we have elected to use the term for ease of distinction between the bodies of scholarship we have explored in this book.

3 AmeriCorps City Year corps members work with the non-profit organization AmeriCorps to provide student, classroom and school-wide support in high-need schools in urban contexts in the US.

4 In New York City, integrated co-teaching classrooms comprise 40% students with
   disabilities and 60% students without disabilities and are collaboratively taught by
   a general education and a special education teacher.

References

Ahmed, S. (2006). *Queer phenomenology: Orientations, objects, others.* Durham, NC: Duke
   University Press.
Ahmed, S. (2010). *The promise of happiness.* Durham, NC: Duke University Press.
Annamma, S. A., Connor, D., & Ferri, B. (2013). Dis/ability critical race studies
   (DisCrit): Theorizing at the intersections of race and dis/ability. *Race Ethnicity and
   Education, 16*(1), 1–31.
Annamma, S., & Morrison, D. (2018). DisCrit classroom ecology: Using praxis to
   dismantle dysfunctional education ecologies. *Teaching and Teacher Education,
   73,* 70–80.
Anzaldúa, G. (1987). *Borderlands, La Frontera: The new mestiza* (3rd ed.). San Francisco:
   Aunt Lute Books.
Ashby, C. (2012). Disability studies and inclusive teacher preparation: A socially just
   path for teacher education. *Research and Practice for Persons with Severe Dis- abilities,
   37*(2), 89–99.
Barad, K. (2007). *Meeting the universe halfway: Quantum physics and the entanglement of
   matter and meaning.* Durham, NC: Duke University Press.
Barad, K. (2008). Posthumanist performativity: Toward an understanding of how matter comes to matter. In S. Alaimo & S. Hekman (Eds.), *Material feminisms* (pp. 120–
   154). Bloomington, IN: Indiana University Press.
Booth, T. (2009). Keeping the future alive: Maintaining inclusive values in educa-
   tion and society. In M. Alur & V. Timmons (Eds.), *Inclusive education across cul-
   tures: Crossing boundaries, sharing ideas* (pp. 121–134). New Delhi: Sage.
Brah, A. (2003). Diaspora, border and transnational identities. In R. Lewis & S. Mills
   (Eds.), *Feminist postcolonial theory: A reader* (pp. 613–634). New York: Routledge.
Braidotti, R. (2018). A theoretical framework for the critical posthumanities. *Theory,
   Culture and Society,* 1–31. Special issue.
Citywide Council on Special Education. (n.d.) *Citywide council on special education: Annual
   report 2010–2011.* New York, NY: Citywide Council on Special Education.
Clandinin, J. (2013). *Engaging in narrative inquiry.* Walnut Creek, CA: Left Coast Press.
Clandinin, D. J., & Connelly, F. M. (2000). *Narrative inquiry: Experience and story in qual-
   itative research.* San Francisco, CA: Joey Bass.
Connor, D. J., Ferri, B. A., & Annamma, S. (Eds.) (2016). *DisCrit: Critical conversations
   around race, class, & disability.* New York, NY: Teachers College Press.
Danforth, S., & Gabel, S. (2006). *Vital questions facing disability studies in education.*
   New York: Peter Lang.

Danforth, S., & Naraian, S. (2015). This new field of inclusive education: Beginning a dialogue on conceptual foundations. *Intellectual and Developmental Disabilities, 53*(1), 70–85.

DeLanda, M. (2006). *New philosophy of society: Assemblage theory and social complexity.* New York, NY: Continuum.

Delgado, R., & Stefancic, J. (2017). *Critical race theory: An introduction.* New York, NY: NYU Press.

Elbaz-Luwisch, F. (2005). *Teachers' voices: Storytelling & Possibility.* Greenwich, CT: IAP.

Ellingson, L. L. (2011). Analysis and representation across the continuum. In N. K. Denzin & Y. S. Lincoln (Eds.), *The Sage handbook of qualitative research* (pp. 595–610). Thousand Oaks, CA: Sage.

Erevelles, N. (2011). *Disability and difference in global contexts: Enabling a transformative body politic.* New York, NY: Palgrave Macmillan.

Feely, M. (2016). Disability studies after the ontological turn: A return to the material world and material bodies without a return to essentialism. *Disability & Society, 31*(7), 863–883.

Frank, A. W. (2010). *Letting stories breathe: A socio-narratology.* Chicago: University of Chicago.

Gabel, S. L. (Ed.) (2005). *Disability studies in education: Readings in theory and method.* New York: Peter Lang.

Hau, C. S. (2000). On representing others: Intellectuals, pedagogy and the uses of error. In P. M. L. Moya & M. R. Hames-Garcia (Eds.), *Reclaiming identity: Realist theory and the predicament of postmodernism* (pp. 133–170). Berkeley, CA: University of California Press.

Hehir, T., Figueroa, R., Gamm, S., Katzman, L. I., Gruner, A., Karger, J., & Hernandez, J. (2005). *Comprehensive management review and evaluation of special education.* The New York City Department of Education. https://www.uft.org/files/attachments/hehir-report.pdf

Holland, D., Lachiotte, Jr., W., Skinner, D., & Cain, C. (1998). *Identity and agency in cultural worlds.* Cambridge, MA: Harvard University Press.

Leonardo, Z., & Broderick, A. (2011). Smartness as property: A critical exploration of intersections between whiteness and disability studies. *Teachers College Record, 113*(10), 2206–2232.

Malagon, M. C., Huber, L., & Velez, V. N. (2009). Our experiences, our methods: Using grounded theory to inform critical race theory methodology. *Seattle Journal for Social Justice 8*(1), 253–272.

Maxwell, J. A. (2012). *A realist approach for qualitative research.* Thousand Oaks, CA: Sage.

Minh-ha, T. T. (2011). *Elsewhere, within here: Immigration, refugeeism and the boundary event.* New York: Routledge.

Mohanty, S. P. (2000). The epistemic status of cultural identity: On *Beloved* and the postcolonial condition. In P. M. L. Moya & M. R. Hames-Garcia (Eds.), *Reclaiming identity: Realist theory and the predicament of postmodernism.* Berkeley, CA: University of California Press.

Mohanty, C. T. (2003). *Feminism without borders: Decolonizing theory, practicing solidarity.* Durham, NC: Duke University Press.

Moya, P. M. L. (2000). Post-modernism, "realism," and the politics of identity: Cherrie Moraga and Chicana feminism. In P. M. L. Moya & M. R. Hames-Garcia (Eds.), *Reclaiming identity: Realist theory and the predicament of postmodernism* (pp. 67–101). Berkeley, CA: University of California Press.

Naraian, S. (2017). Teaching for inclusion: Eight principles for effective and equitable practice. In A. J. Artiles & E. B. Kozleski (Eds.), *Disability, culture and equity* book series. New York, NY: Teachers College Press.

Naraian, S., & Khoja-Moolji, S. (2016). Happy places, horrible times, and scary learners: Affective performances and sticky objects in inclusive classrooms. *International Journal of Qualitative Studies in Education, 29*(9), 1131–1147.

Naraian, S., & Schlessinger, S. (2017). When theory meets the "reality of reality": Reviewing the sufficiency of the social model of disability as a foundation for teacher preparation for inclusive education. *Teacher Education Quarterly, 44*(1), 81-100.

Oyler, C. (2011). Teacher preparation for inclusive and critical (special) education. *Teacher Education and Special Education, 34*(3), 201–218.

Pantic, N. (2015). A model for study of teacher agency for social justice. *Teachers and Teaching, 21*(6), 759–778.

Postma, D. (2016). The ethics of becoming in a pedagogy for social justice: A *posthumanist* perspective. *South African Journal of Higher Education, 30*(3), 310–328.

Priestly, M., Biesta, G., & Robinson, S. (2015). *Teacher agency: An ecological approach.* London, UK: Bloomsbury.

Probyn, E. (2010). Writing shame. In M. Greg & G. J. Seigworth (Eds.), *The affect theory reader* (pp. 71–90). Durham, NC: Duke University Press.

Puar, J. K. (2017). *The right to maim: Debility, capacity, disability.* Durham, NC: Duke University Press.

Roegman, R. (2018). Seen, unseen, and unforeseen dangers: What a white emerging scholar learned about positionality in research with racially diverse practitioners. *International Journal of Qualitative Studies in Education, 31*(9), 836–850.

Scott, J. (2014). Experience. In A. M. Haggar (Ed.), *Just methods: An interdisciplinary feminist reader* (pp. 272–282). Boulder, CO: Paradigm Publ.

Siebers, T. (2008). *Disability theory.* Ann Arbor: University of Michigan Press.

Stone-Mediatore, S. (2000). Chandra Mohanty and the revaluing of experience. In U. Narayan & S. Harding (Eds.), *Decentering the center: Philosophy for a multicultural, postcolonial and feminist world* (pp. 110–127). Bloomington: Indiana University Press.

Vygotsky, L. (1986). *Thought and language.* Cambridge, MA: MIT Press.

Ware, L. (2010). Disability studies in education. In S. Tozer, B. P. Gallegos, A. Henry, M. B. Greiner, & P. G. Price (Eds.), *Handbook of research in the social foundations of education* (pp. 244–260). New York, NY: Routledge.

Watts, I. E., & Erevelles, N. (2004). These deadly times: Reconceptualizing school violence by using critical race theory and disability studies. *American Educational Research Journal, 41*(2), 271–299.

Chapter 1

A Male Teacher of Color: Filling the Void

With Taiyo Ebato

"I really need justice, social justice in my mind, in my mindset, in order to go to work every day ... as the [Special Education] teacher, as the one writing the IEPs[1], as the one differentiating curriculum. That's constantly what I'm trying to do -- ask the students and families, and [for] the parent's voice and the student's voice."

As a soft-spoken member of his cohort, Taiyo could generally be observed listening carefully to his colleagues, his expressive face moving alongside the remarks of his peers. When he spoke, however, it was clear that his restrained manner belied the intensity of his feelings towards inclusive teaching; his ongoing assessment of his own role and his responsibilities to his students were always readily apparent to us. Due to school-related matters, Taiyo was unable to attend two of the six group meetings, but he participated freely in two hour–long interviews during the course of the year. In the following pages, we sift and rummage through those carefully spoken words to surface some tentative narrative threads about Taiyo that can suggest his orientation to inclusive practice. We want to be cautious in our assertions; like the other teachers in this study, our stories about Taiyo are compiled without observing his practice. Even as his words hint at the complexities and struggles that preoccupied him, we do not want to suggest that *our* words in any way produce an account of him that is "true" in some fixed, eternal sense. Rather, we look for the ways in which his own sense-making, via his conversations with us, provokes us to imagine how inclusion may be understood. In other words, his words evoke images of social encounters, times and places that we have tried to assemble as a particular kind of orientation to inclusion that other teachers, and teachers of color, may be able to recognize.

Throughout his conversations with us, Taiyo invoked a commitment to his role as a male teacher of color working with significant numbers of students from Hispanic, Asian-American and African-American communities in a Title 1 high school filled with mostly white teachers. At the time of the study, he served as a special education teacher in this school, working in collaboratively taught classrooms with his general education counterparts. The school was bound by graduation requirements set by the district—namely, successful passage of state-sponsored examinations—which meant that teachers had less flexibility in designing curricular and instructional experiences for their students. Despite this constraint, Taiyo was satisfied, that it was a "progressive" public school that valued the learning of both students and teachers. He co-taught with general educators across ninth, tenth and eleventh grades in History. He was grateful for the school's decision to assign special educators to content areas rather than to students or grade levels. This allowed him to work across grades in a content area he felt comfortable with—History—while other special educators did the same for Science, Math, and English. With the advent of citywide special education reforms, there were increasing numbers of students with disabilities entering this school; most of his students came with the "generic" label of Learning Disabled. Even as most students lived under the poverty line, he described them as "high functioning" and as collectively steering the school toward a competitive environment.

Taiyo was acutely conscious of his unique position in the school.

I'm the only male teacher of color amongst a staff of 30. One of three teachers of color within a staff of 30. And then of course the students with IEPs are predominantly students of color, you know. And, then also me being the basketball coach for the JV team, which is the ninth and tenth graders, the majority of the basketball team are men of color, young men of color. So, all these things I feel like--I'm, you know, *I see the void and I'm trying to fill it.*

Recognizing that students lived in a "culturally segregated world"—borne out readily in the ways different groups gathered together separately for lunch at school—he took seriously his mission to advocate for the students, to serve as an exemplar for them and to "offer an alternative every day as an educator." Taiyo's expressed commitment to these students has been documented among justice-oriented teachers of color (Burciaga & Kohli, 2018; Kohli & Pizarro, 2016). Such work has been described as largely invisible. In situating our narrative of Taiyo as a first-year teacher within this important dimension, we want to avoid a similar oversight of the kinds of competencies brought by teachers of color. Simultaneously, and in keeping with this chapter's focus on lived contradictions, we noticed that, just as much of the literature on Culturally Responsive Pedagogy has not attended sufficiently to the ableist underpinnings of monocultural schooling (Blanchett, Klinger, & Harry, 2009; Borrero, Flores, de la Cruz, 2016), Taiyo's stories also surface this gap. Still, we recognize in his stories the intertwining of ableism and racism that DisCrit scholarship has unequivocally established (Annamma, Ferri, & Connor, 2018).

In the following pages, we trace some strands within the mission Taiyo set out for himself.

Recognition

Research has shown that the identities of teachers of color are inseparable from how they envision the role and responsibilities of teachers; "they see themselves and their families reflected in their students and feel a responsibility to support and serve them" (Kohli & Pizarro, 2016, p. 77). In the particular mix of race/ethnicities that comprised this school, Taiyo recognized his own status as a person of color, as being "valuable." In fact, when considering this school as a potential site for employment, he hoped that this status would be recognized by the administration, too, as an asset. Taiyo's determination to heighten his connection to his students (which might implicitly emphasize their *disconnection* from other teachers) was undoubtedly stimulated by a desire for his students to affirm their racial/ethnic identities and develop a healthy sense of themselves given their subordinate cultural position in the school. After all, "to be denied recognition—or to be 'misrecognized'—is to suffer both a distortion of one's relation to one's self and an injury to one's identity (Fraser, 2000). For Taiyo, the *recognition* of a shared cultural identity referenced a life-altering necessity that could not be fulfilled by a white teacher: "as great of a teacher that a white teacher can be, [many] students kind of need this other thing where they need to be reflected, you know?" Taiyo was noting the particular social context of this school where the routine appearance of a teacher which may otherwise be insignificant, could produce profound effects because of its capability to materialize other types of bodies.

Yet, such recognition also transcended the immediacy of place and time. "And, when they see me it's like they also see a teacher, but they also see an older version of themselves. That kind of feeling happens often and it's kind of this very almost palpable exchange that happens." The viscerally experienced encounter with Taiyo who mirrored their "otherness," fueled, for his students, the possibility of other ways of knowing themselves both at this moment and in the future. Such a generative movement in time that marked these "palpable exchange[s]" was no less significant for Taiyo. His own memories of his racial/ethnic status surfaced in the significance he attached to these exchanges with his students. The memory of the significance of his own teacher's receptivity to his desire for discussion around troubling political events intensified the shared recognition of "otherness" with his current students. He knew that the negative incarnations of such "otherness"—being "shut down" or "angered, embittered … and antagonistic about school and education"—could be mitigated by a teacher. Such memories drove the desire in him for the opportunity to mitigate that process for these students.

In these and other past events (he also recalled the dubious distinction of being the student of color on a scholarship at an elite private high school), he recognized his own life-experience as fostering the "asset perspective" that he brought to his practice as an educator.

It fostered an awareness of the symbolic "intersectional space" that he embodied for his students straddling knowledges of both their school and home communities, while also serving as their springboard for their "next destination point." Collectively, it allowed him to engage in a practice of "authentic caring" (Kohli & Pizarro, 2016) that was holistic in its outlook and which went beyond concern for the academic progress of his students. He saw his own well-being as inextricably linked with that of his students.

The experience of recognition also meant that students sometimes came to know him better than his colleagues. Despite his reticence—"I am not someone who talks about myself all the time"—he noted that within just a few weeks, his students came to learn about his own interest in art. He attributed their ability to glean this knowledge about him to that "intangible" shared connection between him and them; a connection that spanned both home and school communities. "Filling the void" of non-recognition for his students also meant filling the voids of *mis-recognition* that his colleagues might unintentionally create. For instance, when an overnight field trip was being planned, he was assigned to supervise two boys of color who had, at that time, developed "antagonistic relationships" with other students and teachers. Fully aware that he was "stuck" with these boys "for a reason," Taiyo was not critical of such moves. On the contrary, he spoke glowingly of how the students "shined" and "blossomed" on the trip. Recognition transformed the bodies of his students, as it did his. *His* recognition that students of color were some of the students in the school that "teachers and schools have the hardest time with" attached itself firmly to his own mission as a male teacher of color in this context, deepening his commitments to being a particular kind of teacher.

"Filling in the voids" for his students also meant that he had to manage the absence of recognition *he* experienced within this community. Inasmuch as the recognition he shared with his students produced an embodied sense of connection, the *absence* of such recognition with his mostly white colleagues, produced an equally embodied sense of discomfort. Having lived among diverse communities for most of his life, finding himself in a space now which was mostly white, was different this time: "It's not like I'm sweating my palms about it but it's something that's a little out of my comfort zone." The racially marked social distance between his colleagues and himself, coupled with his zeal to fill in the void for his students of color exerted a particular weight on him that could materialize physically.

Taiyo expressed a stance of relational accountability (Kohli & Pizarro, 2016) to his students and their communities. He understood students' lives as grounded in community cultural wealth (Yosso, 2005) and sought to affirm that in as many ways as he could. As the following section discloses, this commitment to his students simultaneously invoked a recognition of community as a form of living. It was this which prompted him to determinedly join his colleagues on social occasions such as "happy hour," even if he felt experientially disconnected from them. In this and other instances where he acknowledged the difficult or uncomfortable steps one must take to the "to get through to the other side," we see Taiyo inhabiting the borderland spaces that mark the tensions between upholding commitments to equity and engaging with dominant systems to move towards change (Anzaldúa, 1987).

Inclusion, Community and Change

Though he did not differentiate among the racial/ethnic groups of students he served, Taiyo's unabashed preoccupation with his identity as a person of color within this setting did not resemble an unrefined identity politics. We have suggested that Taiyo's orientation to his students was interwoven with his orientation to community. Burciaga and Kohli (2018) illustrated that teachers of Color struggled to enact a stance of community relationality with their students because of a deficit-oriented school culture that was expressed in mainstream ways of understanding racial/ethnic differences or via an ethos of standardization. Unlike those participants, Taiyo was not unaware of the misrecognition (Fraser, 2000) extended by other teachers. He deployed his awareness of these gaps in the school to enrich the school community. In other words, his affirmative orientation to the students of color in this school operated simultaneously as an orientation of positivity to the larger school community itself. In this section, we document the particular ways Taiyo's location within communities of Color allowed him to imagine and enact an inclusive community.

Notwithstanding the lack of diversity in its staff, Taiyo was still drawn by the intensely positive environment at the school. Its "positive staff culture" where members loved teaching, and where the ethos bespoke a "passion" for "intellectualism," induced him to remain, even as he worried about the disconnect between himself and his colleagues. His appreciation of its positive culture transferred to how he understood the work of inclusion happening in the school. He could describe the school approvingly as "transitioning to be more inclusive" and as sincerely taking up the directives via the district-wide special education reforms to produce meaningful outcomes. Clearly, there were different understandings of inclusion at the school, but for the large part, he felt convinced that people were making genuine attempts to support students.

Taiyo's generous orientation to the school's efforts towards inclusion may owe in some part to his own acknowledgement of it as a process of change and transformation. The district-wide special education reforms that called for more students with disabilities to be educated alongside their general education peers had set the process irrevocably in motion. Yet, in Taiyo's account, the fundamental changes that were being wrought owed not only to district mandates but to the students themselves. As he remarked: "If you look at it in a dialectical way, they're actually the ones who are changing the group. They're actually the ones who are changing public education because the curriculum doesn't always fit them." This unrecognized agentic capability of the students (typically students with labeled disabilities) to bring about change in the system further fueled his excitement about being a special education teacher at this time.

Taiyo's faith in the capability of students with disabilities to shift the culture and practice of education traveled alongside his recognition of historically-mediated understandings that inevitably characterize processes of change. Like other schools in the district, this school was co-located with another in the same building. In the collective memory of building personnel, comparisons that worked to the disadvantage of some students marked how inclusion came to be understood in this school.

> And the security guards and the janitorial staff, they've been there for all 15 years or so [since] it's been open. And so, apparently there's this joke amongst them, one of the head custodians, that, that Baron Hill Prep is becoming more like the last school.

This cautionary, even dismissive stance of the building workers portended a negative process of "becoming" that took its form via both uncharitable jokes and more serious observations from the current principal about "a lot more behavior issues and disciplinary issues because of the newer population." When recounting these stories, Taiyo was clearly uncomfortable, but he could also see that some of the struggles for inclusion originated in a "fear and panic" in teachers, alongside other more "legitimate" struggles that had to do with the ways in which some teachers remained unsupported by the school structure. Other fears that the school was "regressing" because of these students, were simply too irrational to be admissible and Taiyo laughingly dismissed them: "I don't know what to say to all of that." Taiyo's view of these struggles for inclusion was unfinalized and open-ended. Between ludicrous arguments and other excessively broad claims that students with learning differences had always been part of the school, he recognized that "somewhere in there, is the truth."

Taiyo's orientation to the possibility of sincerity in the school's efforts towards inclusion carried forward his understanding of change as fundamental to inclusion. In the following excerpt, he described the shift in his colleague's thinking. This teacher had likely taught for 20 years and served at Baron Hill Prep for about 11 years. At the beginning of the year, he spoke "very critically, almost in a kind of mean way" about a student with a labeled disability whose literacy levels compared poorly with that of her grade-level peers.

> But, you know, [given] the environment of the school and the classes, by midway to the end of the year, I mean he really loved this student because even though this student really struggled with basic literacy skills, she was such a critical thinker. And especially in discussions, and in class, she was just so brilliant and bright that, you know, by midway of the year it's like this student helped change the way he thought about students like her.

Characteristically missing in Taiyo's description was his own intervention in bringing about the shift. Instead, Taiyo presented the change as being wrought by a particular kind of environment and by the student herself. In fact, the glow from the transformative impact on the teacher, attached itself to the student whose "brilliance" and "brightness" far exceeded the value of proficiency in basic academic skills. Taiyo affirmed the value and necessity of his colleagues' growth as well as the capability of students to participate actively in that process. In his account, the school, the student and the teacher were all agentic in the process of change (DeLanda, 2006)

Although Taiyo rarely attached praise to his own efforts, he did recognize himself as similarly enmeshed within that process of change, particularly through the tools that could serve him. One tool that he recognized as facilitating his change-making efforts was the language acquired through his teacher preparation program which allowed him to articulate his ideas about learning in ways that could raise his credibility with the administration and his colleagues. As change-maker on a large scale, Taiyo ultimately sought more collective organizing around issues that could produce broader changes in schools, such as the focus on standardization imposed on schools via mandated high-stakes state-sponsored examinations. In desiring to organize around broader issues of accountability that can bring together multiple groups of like-minded educators, Taiyo disclosed a coalitional stance (Sandoval, 2000; Mohanty, 2003) that readily resembled Third Space practitioners (English, 2005). His orientation surfaced the complexities of relationships in school, where commitments rarely operate separately, but which are instead, entangled with each other.

Enacting a Colleague of Color: "Just Have People's Good Intentions First."

As suggested in the preceding pages, Taiyo's appropriation of his role as a teacher of color surfaced particular orientations to knowing his community. It afforded him a vantage point to "notice the ways in which a lot of teachers just connect[ed] with each other automatically."

He tried conscientiously to deepen his connections with colleagues who appeared to move in worlds different from his own, as they lived their "white picket suburban lives," coming into the city to teach urban youth. He recognized them as "well-meaning" even as he simultaneously wondered about the "long-term sustainability of being in a place where I may not always connect with my colleagues." The ambivalence inherent in Taiyo's dilemma of belonging within this professional community—his connection to students but not to teachers, could not ultimately be generative professionally—grew into a determination to strengthen his students' understanding of race relations.

Scholars have noted the affordances of a position of marginality that allows a unique and often unexplored perspective on mainstream experiences (Collins, 2000; Mohanty, 2003). Being "the only one in mostly white circles, or the only one in mostly black and Latino circles," for much of his life, conferred particular advantages, because by the time he became an adult, he "felt very equipped to be in whatever circle." Perhaps it was this familiarity with being an "outsider within" (Collins, 2000) that permitted Taiyo to extend an empathetic orientation to his colleagues, understanding their efforts towards inclusion as well-meaning and sincere. In other words, in Taiyo's description of the ongoing work of inclusion within his school, his commitment to equity moved alongside an affinity with his colleagues, even if they might sometimes be at odds with each other. He was not unaware of the ableism that permeated some of their practices; still, he also seemed to keep open the possibility of change. The "myths" or "weird habits" that seemed to circulate among his colleagues—usually pertaining to student capability—did not prevent him from acknowledging them as generally caring and "reflective" teachers who were "super dedicated in their own ways." His orientation to teachers presumed good intentions and acknowledged their misses or slips as stemming from ignorance.

A positive orientation to his colleagues' good intentions freed Taiyo to take his own risks as a first-year teacher in approaching the largely white faculty on matters of race. His recognition of students' need to engage in conversation about recent racially charged events prompted him to initiate a conversation with the faculty about this issue and to share curricular resources that his colleagues might find useful. Taiyo reported that his action produced a "whole chain" of events/conversation that generated thanks and greater collegiality. Emboldened by the response, he continued to initiate such conversations, discovering that his colleagues welcomed them and may have themselves been inhibited by some "element of fear" in engaging such conversations. Characteristically, he remained conscious of his obligations to both: "I'm conscious of not being so student-centered that I completely share all of the connections with the students, and not empathize equally with the adults in the building as well." Taiyo's orientations to his students and to teachers deposited him in an in-between space, (Minh-Ha, 2011) between two extremes as he illustrates above, that still did not appear to have compromised his understanding of his role as a critically conscious teacher, but rather, seemed to flow from it.

It also meant that that he needed to use his own relationships with students in measured ways. Supremely aware of the power he wielded as a favored teacher to whom students freely expressed attachment, he felt compelled to check their public displays of favoritism towards him in the interest of squelching negative feelings from his colleagues. Yet, the strength derived from those relationships also afforded him a comfortable location from which to mentor a new co-teacher who, arriving from an affluent suburban location, expressed little understanding of the lives of majority of the students in this building. The latter's militaristic approach to relationships with students quickly resulted in instability in the classroom. Taiyo's positive orientation to his school community transferred to his mentoring style, enabling him to express care for his new co-teacher's progress, despite the unusual power dynamics that structured their work relations (both were new teachers at the school). His biases towards his students clearly evident, he could characterize his new colleague thus: "Even though he comes from that kind of culture, he definitely wants to improve. He really wants to grow." Taiyo's efforts on behalf of his students *required* that he understand teachers also as learners.

Diversity Pedagogy

Whether with teachers or with students, the political nature of his work was always evident to us, and we suspect, to Taiyo himself. This is hardly surprising given the professional identity that he had taken up in this particular school. The following threads of practice that we gleaned from his work are all grounded in his particular attachments to the students in this school as students from minoritized communities learning with/from a predominantly white faculty.

Taiyo sought a pedagogy of community that could account for the myriad states of health, learning and needs expressed by the student body. In that regard, he could not emphasize enough the importance of circles as a routine practice in schools. Understanding it as an "ancient" practice, he believed there was something "profound" and "powerful" about doing circles. While on a pragmatic level the practice of circles inculcated skills of empathy, for him, its real power stemmed from its capability to heal a community. Taiyo's history with the practice of circles was rooted in his own beginnings as a teacher—when he taught poetry as an 18-year-old to urban youth. It was the affective possibilities invoked by the practice of circles via poems, songs, stories, etc. that materialized its power to heal and hold a community together.

> When we all learned that our student was found dead, and we shared that news, it was the circles that saved us. It was telling them I love them that saved us. It was talking openly about healing trauma that saved us. It was sharing poems and songs and stories, testimonies, that saved us.

Taiyo's reliance on circles as a routine practice to "save" his community renders the mental health of his students (and by extension the school community) as existing in a fragile state and as requiring a deliberate and intentional effort to preserve it. But he, too, was not separable from such an existential condition of fragility and referred to the circles, as "my therapy." The restorative effects of this practices were no less relevant for his own state of being within the school. It was no wonder then that, if he was unable to do this every Friday with his students, it just "didn't feel right."

Implicitly, the practice of circles permitted Taiyo to practice a pedagogy of love with his students. A natural extension of this could be found in his attachment to coaching as an additional way to reach his students. A practice that he had always wanted to try, coaching offered a space freed from the constraints of classroom cultural dynamics allowing him to do the work of relationship-building. Coaching, however, was not quite a neutral terrain and Taiyo was aware of its political force in this particular racialized context. It presented as an additional opportunity to mentor students, mostly boys of color, many of whom connected poorly with their other teachers in school. Importantly, there were also material successes; under his mentorship, the school won more games than they ever had in its history.

Taiyo prioritized methods in his classes that departed from traditional text-heavy approaches that made it monotonous both for himself and the students. Instead, he paid particular attention to drawing on multiple modalities—"a work of art or, you know, a film clip or a piece of music"—that might allow students different routes to entering the same content. He cared about holistic assessments that could be meaningful for students and called for structures to be put in place to facilitate immediate and thoughtful feedback as a component of grading practices.

Embedded within a curricular context that was bound by the state-sponsored high school examinations, Taiyo sought various ways to invoke its political/cultural dimensions whenever possible to afford his students an alternative entry. For example, this might mean making specific references to the sugar plantations when addressing the topic of Spanish colonization to enable his Latino students to find an "immediate cultural connection," or explicitly making connections to dehumanization and resistance in addressing the Trans-Atlantic Slave trade, or using the writings of people of color when teaching poetry lessons. Taiyo was equally aware that, despite evoking deep student engagement, these curricular interventions were minimal, the "tippety top of the iceberg," when given the reach of the state-sponsored examination curricula. "At the end of the day, when it pops up on the [test], it's like one question, do you know what I mean?" What would/could students remember?

The state-sponsored exam remained a persistent threat that endangered the well-being of his students and obstructed his mission to help them imagine their lives otherwise. Taiyo's own inability to derive meaning from the largely Eurocentric curriculum of the test configured it as the "enemy" evoking strong feelings of mistrust. He considered it to be only marginally improved from his own curricular experiences as a student. The antagonism generated by such mandated curriculum spread to become his frustration in being unable to work towards larger goals for his students. As he pointed out: "It's like teaching them how to fit in a box ... whereas [I want] to teach them how to imagine a different shape, you know?"

Yet, Taiyo was not unaware of the necessity to prepare his students for the high-stakes tests and to do that well. His commitments to his students did not obscure his pragmatism. He recognized the significance of "critical pedagogy, post-structuralism and all of that" which was "powerful", "beautiful" and "great." Still, "teaching explicit test taking skills—It has its place, if that's a loophole that needs to be taken and leaped through, to get there." He worried about the practices of standardization in schools as well as in higher education and was fully cognizant of the profit-making industry they fed. However, even as he hoped for larger scale organizing that could bring about fundamental changes, at this juncture he was inclined to believe that it was still something "that you need to get through." Taiyo's simultaneous endorsement and distrust of accountability practices is not surprising; they reflect the inherent contradictions in taking up inclusive practices (Naraian, 2014). They reflect the fluidity of movement between multiple ideological attachments that leave open the possibility that all points of view can be changed. The "dialectical" relationship he recognized between the students and the school may well characterize his own relationship with his practice.

Taiyo: Five Years Later

Being the only male teacher of color at Baron Hill Prep and being one of the few teachers of color and not "white passing," the connection I had with students was unique. For many of the Asian-American youth, I was likely one of the only Asian-American teachers they have ever had. Most of the student body at the time was of color, particularly of Asian descent and came from low-income families.

In 2014, the way I was treated by students was first like a teacher, but because of my positionality, also like an older family member. By the 2016– 2017 school year, however, the demographics of the high school had shifted from being majority low-income students of color in the upper grades to majority white and middle class in the lower grades. It was a microcosm of gentrification in this community school that historically served students in the Lower East Side, Chinatown, Murray Hill, Upper East Side and East Harlem. Ableism and colorism intersected in schools like this where students with disabilities usually comprised the students of color with darker hues. But by 2016, even the students with disabilities were mostly white in those lower grades.

During the 2016–2017 school year, Trump was also elected president. The school community, for the most part, mourned this event. We circled up in advisory classes the day after the elections, and our students of color and female students in particular processed their fears and grief over the safety of their new national climate. About a month later, like other schools around the country during this time, we entered Baron Hill Prep one morning to see a section of a hallway vandalized with white supremacist iconography by an anonymous student or students, the letters "KKK" cutting across jaggedly. Teachers were saddened and enraged. Some students blamed the younger and whiter grade levels. The anonymity of it was a form of cowardice, but its impact was present. Teachers remarked that a chapter in the life of the school had closed, and a new one began. The Obama era optimism I came in with teaching here had morphed into a need for self-preservation and psychic safety.

During that school year, after three consecutive years of teaching state-mandated exams in social studies, I became disillusioned by attempting to subvert their banking pedagogy. One afternoon, I completed an informal study of a 2014 US history state exam. Out of a required 100 tasks to complete (multiple choice and/or written response), I took note of how many questions and prompts it would require for a student to have learned and memorized people and/or events that necessitated people of color and women. In this particular exam, 95 of the 100 tasks required the memorization of white male names and actions or events where white men were central to its narrative. In other words, a student taking this exam need not know the name or event involving one person of color or woman to receive a 95% on this test. Upon completing my informal study, I felt an indignant clarity, and I knew that I was morally and intellectually against these state exams. Whatever supplementary and modified ethnic studies curriculum I gave at a school like Baron Hill Prep was ultimately delivered alongside a standardized Euro-centric master narrative. I began articulating that for my own long-term sustainability I needed to surround myself with a community of pedagogues who had a deeper analysis of white supremacy culture and the critical tools needed to undo its damage.

As an inclusion teacher at Baron Hill Prep, I saw first-hand how the sys-temic racism of a school's admissions policy, staff hiring practices, curriculum, and a subscription to an elitist state exam created tremendous isolation for stu-dents of color with disabilities, in particular. During my last couple months at this school, I was teaching a unit on writing and delivering speeches. One day while workshopping, the seniors of color, who were mostly students with IEPS, braved their vulnerability with tears in their eyes and shared how they've felt stigmatized and marginalized their entire time as students there, how they were consistently stereotyped as "slower" and full of "behavior problems" being in the ICT classes. I knew I did my best in creating a safe, third space for them to succeed and graduate in this element, but I knew in this moment, too, that I could no longer justify teaching at a school system like this one. I was aware I was "tracked" with them, always teaching classes with this particular group of students of color with disabilities as they moved up in grades. I subverted every measure of the administration's attempts for me to "police" them through humane teaching, but how the larger school community saw and treated them created damage I couldn't contain.

Today in 2019, I teach at a consortium transfer school in a neighboring district. We are part of a network and movement of public schools that have opted out of state exams as graduation assessments through successful lobby-ing for portfolio-based assessments as more complete measures of evaluation. Culturally responsive pedagogy, restorative practices and shared leadership are some of our central community agreements and theories of action. Our staff is intentionally mostly people of color. Furthermore, as a transfer school we intake students who have been pushed out of other schools much like Baron Hill Prep. Our smaller, supportive environment produces graduates out of those most *greatly impacted by the "school-to-prison and deportation pipeline"—students formerly incarcerated, homeless youth, foster care youth, students with disabilities, students of color, immigrant students, and LGBTQIA students. We are their last stop before they completely drop out of high school or age out into GRE programs. Like anywhere, we are a work in progress, but it is in this school where teaching for inclusion, justice and liberation has felt most responsive. I have adopted a newer identity as a mentor to younger teachers of color that has given me unexpected meaning and fulfillment. I acknowledge I still work for the very state that produces the exclusion needed for the existence of a transfer consortium school, but I am more engaged and intellectually sharper, my mindset of justice unscathed and protected.*

Note

1 Individualized Educational Program, a legally mandated document (and process) in the US to ensure that students with disabilities receive a fair and appropriate education.

References

Annamma, S. A., Ferri, B. A., & Connor, D. J. (2018). Disability critical race theory: Exploring the intersectional lineage, emergence, and potential futures of DisCrit in education. *Review of Research in Education*, 42(1), 46–71.

Anzaldúa, G. (1987). *Borderlands, La Frontera: The new mestiza* (3rd ed.). San Francisco: Aunt Lute Books.

Blanchett, W. J., Klingner, J. K., & Harry, B. (2009). The intersection of race, culture, language and disability: Implications for urban education. *Urban Education*, 44, 389–409.

Borrero, N. E., Flores, E., & de la Cruz, G. (2016). Developing and enacting culturally relevant pedagogy: Voices of new teachers of color. *Equity & Excellence in Education*, 49(1), 27–40.

Burciaga, R., & Kohli, R. (2018). Disrupting whitestream measures of quality teaching: The community cultural wealth of teachers of color. *Multicultural Perspectives*, 20(1), 5–12.

Collins, H. P. (2000). *Black feminist thought*. New York: Routledge.

DeLanda, M. (2006). *New philosophy of society: Assemblage theory and social complexity*. New York, NY: Continuum.

English, L. M. (2005). Third-space practitioners: Women educating for justice in the global south. *Adult Education Quarterly*, 55(2), 85–100.

Fraser, N. (2000). Rethinking recognition. *New Left Review, 3,* 107–130.

Kohli, R., & Pizarro, M. (2016). Fighting to educate our own: Teachers of color, relational accountability, and the struggle for racial justice. *Equity & Excellence in Education, 49*(1), 72–84.

Minh-ha, T. T. (2011). *Elsewhere, within here: Immigration, refugeeism and the boundary event.* New York: Routledge.

Mohanty, C. T. (2003). *Feminism without borders: Decolonizing theory, practicing solidarity.* Durham, NC: Duke University Press.

Naraian, S. (2014). Agency in real time? Situating teachers' efforts towards inclusion in the context of local and enduring struggles. *Teachers College Record, 116*(6), 1–38.

Sandoval, C. (2000). *Methodology of the oppressed.* Minneapolis: University of Minnesota Press

Yosso, T. J. (2005). Whose culture has capital? A critical race theory discussion of community cultural wealth. *Race Ethnicity and Education, 8*(1), 69–91.

Chapter 2

Negotiating the Cruel Optimisms of Inclusivity

With Molly Goodell

"If inclusivity is possible, I definitely don't know how to do it."

When Molly entered her graduate program, she was fresh from her undergraduate degree. Her head filled with poststructural theory, she was ready to prove that Foucauldian analysis was not futile, as some educational scholars have suggested, but rather a potential catalyst for dismantling oppressive structures of schooling. As a young, white, cisgender, woman, Molly had come to her commitment to inclusive education as an act of social justice through her philosophical understanding of difference. When introduced to disability studies in education, she quickly attached to this framework; it seemed to speak to the philosophical and social commitments that she held and to her stance on equity and social justice. She was ready to be an inclusive educator, at least ideologically.

The story of her first year of teaching demonstrates the struggles of "becoming" an inclusive educator within a context that did not support the work of inclusivity. It is also a story that sheds light on the ways in which Molly's "becoming" an inclusive educator was marked by her own internal tensions and attachments to success and goodness as a White, able-bodied teacher negotiating a complex and inequitable system of education. She was conscious that at her "very diverse" school, she didn't "contribute to the diversity." Laughing quietly, she noted, "Most people look like me. Lots of like high 20s, low 30s white women," and as her laughter suggests, she was not completely comfortable with this dynamic. Molly's "becoming" then is characterized by affective attachments to her ideological commitments, mediated in part by an intersectional understanding of her identity in relation to her students as individuals with disabilities. She moved through the school year continually seeking a solid ground to stand on, seeking the "right way" to be a social-justice-oriented, inclusive educator. Molly's "becoming" can in many ways be understood as navigating the cruel optimisms of teaching for social justice in a school and societal context that is designed to perpetuate a status quo, as the pursuit of a desire that actually impeded her achievement of that desire (Berlant, 2011). In this way, her desire, her affective attachment, provides some insight into the depth and complexity of her "becoming" beyond the ideological commitments required by a disability studies informed teacher stance. Affect theory is concerned with "forces of encounter" experienced through often subtle intensities in the body that move us to act (Seigworth & Gregg, 2010, p.2). These intensities, sometimes understood as feelings or emotions, operate adjacent to and interacting with conscious thought, informing our ways of being and "becoming". They are as integral to understanding Molly's "becoming" as her conscious and rational thoughts and decisions.

The Promise of Happiness in Inclusive Practice

Molly's understanding of inclusivity was derived from the strong post-structural theoretical focus within her undergraduate education and her introduction to disability studies in education (DSE) in her graduate program. Her ideal conception of inclusion was a classroom where "there doesn't need to be specific accommodations for a specific type of person because everything is just so naturally inclusive and wonderful and happy." Drawing on her understanding of structural inequities and exclusion in schools, she understood her role as the special educa-tion counterpart in the co-teaching relationship, to be the facilitator or even creator of classrooms where all students had equitable access to all content at all times, thus minimizing the necessity to modify or accom-modate for any specific learning need or difference. The better Molly worked to create this accessible space that required as few accommo-dations as possible, the closer to "inclusive and wonderful and happy" the classroom would be, and the more successful she could feel as an inclusive educator. Ahmed (2010) suggests that we move towards or away from particular objects because of their presupposed connection to particular affects or emotions—the ways that make us feel. We move towards that which will make us feel good, that is, towards desire, and away from pain. Inclusivity as an enactment of social justice had a par-ticular pull for Molly. It was a promise of the happy classroom, a way to do social-justice education, and a way to be a "good" and successful teacher—a good White, female, cisgendered, able-bodied teacher—to her students who were less privileged than her. Inclusivity promised the happiness of the social justice educator who could provide equitable learning experiences to all of her students in her classroom.

While positioning herself as an inclusive educator could make Molly feel good about herself, the seeming impossibility of this ideal-ized notion of inclusivity also seemed to move her away from the prac-tice and commitment to inclusivity itself. In recent years it has been well documented that there is a tension between the neoliberal, competitive, test-driven, standardized system of schooling that exists in US schools and the fundamental tenets of inclusivity (Naraian & Schlessinger, 2017; Schlessinger, 2018). Molly clearly felt her own version of this same tension, sharing that "last year [when she was a pre-service student], if I read about someone doing what I'm doing right now, I would have all these things to say about it, about how problematic it is." What she had learned previously about enacting inclusivity could not be reconciled with her actual daily experience in school evoking a clear discomfort. For example, if a student was struggling in a class, Molly felt torn about whether she should be "advocating for a kid to get evaluated versus advocating for them to be without an IEP." At the time of her gradua-tion from her teacher preparation program, she knew that she would likely have readily advocated against the use of IEPs. However, the more she experienced the realities of her school and her students' difficulties with school, she seemed more inclined to appreciate the value of students getting evaluated for additional supports. She shared that she had "found so many things that could go either way" and that it all felt "contradictory" and "disconnected".

Additionally, Molly's concept of a curricular approach and lesson design that could account for all differences and be made accessible for every student was proving to be not only unrealistic, but also not even desirable. The class curriculum often used texts that "a lot of kids just didn't read because they couldn't, they just didn't do well with" them. Molly had to "really fight hard" for any changes to the curriculum, which felt frustrating given that so many students were evidently not engaged with the text. Not only was it difficult to make these types of changes, Molly found that when she was able to use a different text with some students, she was better able to provide the literacy supports that they needed. Separating students with disabilities seemed to be the best way to support them. She moved from "wanting to really merge the Special Ed with Gen Ed" to "whereas now I'm like: Oh, my god. Wait. No. We need to separate them more because so many kids aren't getting what they need." Given the tension between the ideals of inclusion she upheld and the reality of her context, Molly often felt unsuccessful and incompetent sharing that "sometimes I don't know what to advocate for, I don't know what the best thing for them is." She felt a need to "take a major step back from curriculum planning" and "focus more on building (her) knowledge base" to support specific learning needs.

Ideally for her, if she could get this inclusivity "thing" right, she wouldn't have to provide so many accommodations. To have to do so, then, was experienced as a failure to teach inclusively on her part. The only way for her to provide the supports that her students needed seemed to be through separation and accommodations—the antithesis of her idealized inclusive classroom. And so, for every day that a student did not understand the text that the class was reading, Molly felt unsuccessful. The discomfort of failure emerged as resentment (she required more authority to modify for her students with disabilities), as insecurity (she was neither an expert in knowing what her students needed nor was she able to "do inclusivity" with fidelity to the concept), and then again as resentment (shouldn't her teacher education program have prepared her for this better?). In aching for "best practices" to follow, Molly was certain in those first months that "if (inclusivity) is possible, I definitely don't know how to do it." And so, with some self-critique and shame at failing to live up to the ideal of an imagined inclusive educator (Probyn, 2005), Molly proceeded to rethink her pedagogical approaches, pull out more small groups, and do more one-to-one work with students. In doing so, Molly was able to feel more successful in reaching her students, even as she perhaps felt less successful in her achievement of inclusivity.

The Cruel Optimism of Capacity Orientation: Shiny *Ugly* Objects

Molly's ideological struggle with herself was not isolated to the enactment of inclusive teaching; it also emerged in her understandings of the concept of disability. For Molly, part of her attachment to a classroom/world without accommodation as "happy" was derived from the notion that providing accommodations necessitated marking individual students as "other". This marking of the "other" legitimized hierarchized understandings of race, ability, intellectualism, language, and so on. As she began her teaching career she had learned and believed that "disability" was "not a real thing;" rather, it was "just a social construct." She shared that what she "took away [from her graduate education] was that disabilities are not real things and the world, society, should just naturally accommodate difference." In other words, accommodations were necessary in a world that recognized only one way of being human as normal, and other ways as abnormal and requiring adjustment or fixing to conform to normalcy. If we designed a world (in this case a classroom) that did not present barriers to participation for anyone, we would not project a hierarchy of human experience. And so, as Molly began teaching, she was determined to not merely understand her students by the disabilities described on their IEPs. Rather, she was committed to holding a capacity orientation toward her students, to seeing them holistically, and to recognizing their contributions to the classroom community. As a special educator in a system that necessitated this labeling and sorting of students, Molly, not surprisingly, found herself frequently uncomfortable with the way students with disabilities were seen and talked about, and with her own discomfort in knowing how to participate (or not) in these conversations and practices without losing her commitments and harming her students.

Historically and contemporarily, disability has been marked by notions of shame and deviance that have been attached to people with disabilities (Garland-Thomson, 2017). Alongside those notions, come the affective push and pull towards and away from individuals with disabilities because of their perceived deviance. Disability studies scholars have surfaced a range of affects attached to individuals with disabilities: repulsion because of embodied differences and/or intellectual differences; fetishization of these very same differences; and savior complexes over the individuals who display these differences. In the United States, from the late 1800s all the way up through the 1970s there were so-called "ugly laws" on the books in various states that prohibited individuals with disabilities from being seen publicly, and mingling with the general population, unless it was to provide entertainment. The public feeling (Cvetkovitch, 2012) towards disability in this country has been consistently characterized by repulsion—a push away from ugly objects—and fascination—a pull towards shiny ones, those that offer potential for some kind of pleasure. Even as our society has become more inclusive, and individuals can appreciate the problematic ideologies that created these public feelings, such attachments still move in various ways through the individuals who work and have relationships with people with disabilities.

In the case of disability in schooling, we often see teachers moved away from students with disabilities. Teachers rationalize this movement away from a particular population or individual student using a needs-based framework whereby they determine that either they do not have the skill-set to teach the child, or the child simply just does not belong in that particular educational setting. The structures of schooling have been designed to reinforce this exclusionary rationale through a segregated system of special education and the use of a continuum of services that push some bodies further and further toward the margins. In this way, the exclusion of those bodies can also be affectively justified in that it has been rationalized as what is best for the child. This means that the teacher engaged in the act of the excluding can *feel good* about making the decision to segregate a student with a disability .

For Molly, however, her ideological stance complicated her affective response to her students. If students with disabilities were "ugly" objects to be avoided and hidden away by the school system, for Molly they were her shiny objects. She "loved them individually" and felt good about herself as the facilitator of a space where "they have a little bit more freedom to let their freak flags fly." What was categorized by school and society as a negative difference, Molly found compelling for its deviation from the norm. She shared that her students were "the poster children for 'the normal classroom really doesn't work for us'" and that was a foundational piece of her love for them. Affirming the "difference" of her students that was made negatively prominent in school, then, was evocative for Molly. It made her feel good about herself and who she was in relation to her students and in relation to the difference of disability. It allowed Molly to feel she could set herself apart from her colleagues as the representative of, and for, the students with disabilities. For example, when she and her colleagues met as a grade team to discuss individual students, she worried that they did not focus enough on the students with IEPs. Molly was concerned that her colleagues might not see her students with disabilities as students from whom they could learn to inform their overall practice. Being the facilitator of a unique space where their differences were valued created the conditions that allowed Molly to feel good about herself. She felt "effective in that I was able to reach kids on the margins that would not have otherwise [been reached]." Molly's pull towards these students affirmed her own identity as an effective educator. However, it simultaneously created a sort of fetishization of disability that in some ways acted to re-animate an understanding of disability that she was attempting to disrupt.

In her struggle to understand how to enact her capacity orientation in a way that appreciated their contributions and did not stigmatize them through their "difference", Molly initially felt herself actively avoiding naming their *disability* or ability difference. She shared that it felt "wrong to say, 'Hailey has a disability and she needs medication to function in this classroom'." The school context was already guided by deficit thinking; so, to mention disability at all felt to Molly as if she was complicity in that practice. Naming disability felt like participation in deficit thinking, which felt *bad* to Molly. This bad feeling as related to her social justice commitments and personal positioning can be understood as eliciting feelings of shame. As a White, able-bodied woman who was dedicating herself to an inclusivity derived from a progressive theoretical perspective, to knowingly participate in the disability labeling and hierarchization of human difference simply did not sit right in her own body. Probyn (2005) offers that "shame illuminates our intense attachments to the world ... without interest there can be no shame" (P.14). This was why Molly had come to teaching, to disability studies, and to special education; to disrupt this deficit discourse and value the complexities of each individual student. Naming disability felt like a betrayal of that "intense attachment".

It wasn't just the naming of the disability that produced discomfort; it was the requirement to recognize *their* disabilities as necessary for *her öwn* self-perception as an effective educator that felt shameful:

> It feels wrong for Hailey to walk in and I notice she's kind of off and so I ask her if she took her medicine today. And if she says no, it feels wrong for me to then use that as an excuse for why she's not accessing my materials when, like, why can't I modify things so that she can get it in her non-medicated state? Or like, why can't my classroom be different so that it works for her as she is?

It felt wrong, shameful, to use a student's labeled disability to excuse what she perceived as her own inability to reach her students. She attached this shame to her experience of how to be in relation to disability and doubled down on not naming disability. Naming disability not only felt like participating in a deficit driven discourse around "difference," it also felt like blaming her students for something she was conceptualizing as her own shortcomings. The last thing she wanted to do was to become a teacher who blamed her already marginalized students for not performing well enough in her class.

And so, for a while, Molly engaged in a kind of disability-evasiveness, avoiding the use of disability labels and the naming of disability altogether. Annamma, Jackson, and Morrison (2017) use the term "color-evasiveness" to denote a phenomenon intended to support equal access to civil rights wherein " 'race is irrelevant' and therefore, it should be disregarded" (p.147). In a similar vein, Molly appeared to take up a *disability*-evasive approach to support access to classroom participation for *all* of her students. However, much like a color-evasive stance, a disability-evasive approach, even if well-intentioned, "insinuates that recognizing race (or disability) is problematic and therefore the solution is to discount race (or disability)" (Annamma, Jackson, & Morrison, 2017, p.147). In this way, Molly unintentionally affirmed disability as deficient. She felt shame for naming disability in her students, as related to her own desires to be an inclusive social-justice-oriented teacher, and unintentionally ended up suggesting that disability is shameful. This awareness, not surprisingly, also did not sit well with her.

As she moved through her practice, avoiding disability in this way became clearly problematic for her. Logistically, not talking about disabilities was preventing Molly's students from getting the support that they needed from her and from her colleagues. So, avoiding disability moved her away from the shame of supporting a deficit approach to disability, but it simultaneously moved her towards the shame of under-serving her students, and subsequently of feeling unsuccessful as a teacher. She could not hold both commitments—to a capacity orientation and to providing access for all of her students—at the same time with this approach. Steeped in these realities, she determined that "just because it's a social construct, doesn't mean that there's not a real lived experience of someone with disabilities" and that there were real needs that should be supported by schools and teachers.

Beginning to see her students and her work in this new way, Molly was now moved towards a hyper-focus on disability as deficiency, sharing that "the only way I can get what I think my students need, is to be totally conscious of their disability all the time ... like 'Hailey has a disability and needs to be accommodated'." Disability as deficit became productive for Molly in that it gave her ground to stand on to advocate for her students and for herself. She shared that she found it

useful to say "Well, 'this kid has a disability that needs to be accommodated. And without this, he's not going to be able to enjoy school.'"
This *useful*ness, the utility of disability as a deficit, attached a produc-
tivity and a goodness to the disability label itself and moved Molly to
a more nuanced understanding of how to be in relation to disability
labels in her continued commitment to capacity orientation. Not only
did she develop a strategy for "what I can think about when I talk to
students and ... what I now need to bring to the forefront of my mind
when I talk to adults" regarding the significance of the disability label,
her wariness around naming disability dissipated and allowed for a
more holistic appreciative stance toward the complex identities of her
students to emerge. It was as if strategically employing a deficit model
actually supported her evolution toward enacting a capacity orientation with fidelity to her commitments.

The Reflective Teacher and the Productivity of Shame

Molly spent this first year of teaching working diligently to find the
right balance—the promise of happiness—and to arrive at a successful form of inclusive teaching that valued difference with a nuanced
understanding of disability. She did so with a strong understanding
of a disability studies perspective, a genuine commitment to students
with disabilities, and a desire to enact a capacity orientation. And that
was not easy. There were ideological, structural, and curricular issues
that she encountered along the way. Pursuing her desire to be a particular kind of inclusive educator, she continuously repositioned herself,
her students, or her practice in ways that impeded the achievement of
this desire. At times she could rationalize the difficulty of the work and
understand this impediment as inherent in societal discourse itself. But
there was also an embodied experience of her unsuccessful approaches
and ideological missteps; a punch in the gut that triggered disillusionment in the possibilities of inclusivity, disillusionment in herself and
her ability to do this important and necessary work. This shame, that
was evidence of Molly's "intense attachment" (Probyn, 2005, p.15) to
doing right by her students through her work as an inclusive educator,
wore on her, but it did not wear her down.

Probyn (2005) offers that "when we feel shame, it is because our interest has been interfered with, but not canceled out. The body wants to continue being interested, but something happens to 'incompletely reduce' that interest" (p.15). Molly's story can be read as highlighting the difficulty, perhaps even futility, of pursuing inclusivity. It can also be read as the perseverance of a committed educator. Molly continued to revisit her pedagogy, to rethink her ideology, to question herself, and to push herself to do better. Although it was certainly jostled, her attachment to inclusivity was not completely reduced. Molly shared:

> I think at first, I was resentful ... Well, not resentful. But confused by the notion that disability is socially constructed and then also having to deal with that we live in this society that constructed it, so-- it exists. And that, I think, in the beginning, was really hard to navigate and think about, coming right out of grad school. That said, my teaching philosophy or stance grew out of that ... I guess what I'm trying to say is that I think the first couple month period of weird confusion was really helpful in just developing the way I interact with students.

Her shame was discomforting, frustrating, and confusing, but it was also productive in deepening her work. Her shame pushed her to reexamine how to be in relation to disability labels, to disability itself as not-real-but-also-real, and to her own teaching practice as related to both. Her shame pushed her to shift and change her practice in the pursuit of teaching her students, regardless of the systems and structures of her school.

There is something both hopeful and cruel in thinking that the pursuit of inclusivity may necessitate the experience of shame. The pain, embarrassment, disillusionment, and self-loathing that are associated with shame are not desirable feelings. The protective part of our teacher educator selves would, in many ways, hope to prepare new teachers to never have to feel bad, confused, or less than capable in their work. It is also a central tenet of inclusive education that practitioners should be continuously reflective in their ideology and their practice. Molly's experience illustrates that these bad, frustrating, and confusing feelings can actually drive that reflective practice in generative ways. As Molly's professors, we did not fully anticipate and prepare her for the kinds of struggles that she experienced during her first year and her *bad* feelings as she questioned her own capacity. But in working through those feelings she came to her own reflective practice, a deeply embodied reflective practice, that was more sophisticated than what we might have been able to teach her. As Molly completed that year of teaching, she was optimistic; optimistic in knowing that there was not a "right way" to be an inclusive teacher, optimistic that she was developing her philosophy and practice; and optimistic that her experiences, confusion, resentment and all, could and would continue to inspire her to reexamine and reimagine herself, her students, and her practice.

Molly: Five Years Later

In undergrad, I loved Anthropology because it allowed me to stretch my brain philosophically and ideologically; we pulled back to see the big picture of systems and societies, always grounded in the lived experiences of real people.

As a teacher, I am much the same way: a big-picture thinker, driven by the people (my students) that my work is in service of. This is also what I enjoyed about my graduate program. We talked about the system. We talked about practices in schooling through history. Disability Studies aligned so concretely with what I learned in Anthropology. I was ready to read, think, and philosophize about the systems of power, privilege and access so that I could charge into the world and overturn them all.

In my eagerness, I turned complex issues into black and white ones. For "Grad-School Molly," all we had to do was recognize the specific tentacles of the system that hold students back, and work against them. For each point of oppression, we identified in the system, there seemed a clear way forward:

1. *The system focuses on student deficits and lagging skills; as an inclusive educator I'll focus on their strengths.*
2. *The system creates stigmas, low expectations, and lasting negative social-emotional & academic effects by separating students from their grade-level peers. As an inclusive educator, I'll never separate my students based on ability. Ever.*
3. *The system disproportionately labels young men of color with disabilities and funnels them into special education. As an inclusive educator,*

the young men of color on my caseload were probably misdiagnosed and should not have an IEP.

4. *The system uses the medical model of disability to dehumanize and stigmatize. As an inclusive educator, I'll dogmatically abide by the social model of disability.*

5. *Classroom management systems are tools of the oppressor. As an inclusive educator, I'll only use restorative practices.*

Perhaps I first came to understand inclusive education as an act, in service of students with exceptionalities, against a system whose only goal is to stigmatize, dehumanize, and exclude. The vision for my first year was clear. My classroom would be one in which all students could learn. They'd enter our door, leave that oppressive world behind them, and finally feel seen and heard and be able to learn. I leaned in to the ideas that "inclusive teaching is just good teaching" and "all kids want to do well." Behavior management? Nah. "All kids can learn." If I could create the perfect conditions for all the unique learners in my classroom, there would be no need for students to act out. What a happy peaceful environment it would be. Learning would happen.

The tension between my vision of inclusivity and the reality of what I had the skills to do was real. And the shame that I felt not being able to realize this vision was also real. Now, I chuckle at the naivety of that original vision. I'm sure another source of my shame was realizing that my vision was not only impossible but wrong. I had all these ideas of how to be an inclusive educator but couldn't figure out how to enact them. And then, those who were not engaging in these inclusive practices, were beloved and effective teachers!

I'm thankful that my shame seemed to fuel me. At some point, it forced me to admit that I did not actually know everything, and that humility took me even farther. I sought out resources and learned how to be a better literacy teacher, speak confidently about disability labels, and use systems and routines that provided structure without being oppressive. I learned these things from the teachers whose practices "Grad-School Molly" would certainly have labeled oppressive. As I learned from my colleagues, I better saw the complexity in every "truth" about the system.

I have come to understand inclusive teaching to be a perpetual balancing act. Devoid of context, every decision I make can be viewed as just or unjust. Many of the questions I struggled with in my first year remain unanswered.

But, instead of feeling shame, I have come to understand that my job is to grapple with these concerns. From year to year, even from day to day the answers are not the same. As new cohorts of students come in, as students master new skills, as trauma rears its head, our work is to try to walk the perfect line for each student. It's a balancing act in a system that has both exclusionary tendencies and protections for those who struggle most. It requires immense thoughtfulness, social awareness, and humility to build learning partnerships with the students, their families, and other teachers. There is no handbook that will make us champion inclusive educators. It is about building our capacity to think deeply about an individual in the midst of the chaos of teaching and finding ways to leverage the best of what this system has. We can do this by pulling our students and our colleagues close. We can do this with creativity, empathy, humility, openness, and perhaps most importantly, forgiveness of ourselves when we are wrong.

References

Annamma, S. A., Jackson, D. D., & Morrison, D. (2017). Conceptualizing color-evasiveness: Using dis/ability critical race theory to expand a color-blind racial ideology in education and society. *Race Ethnicity and Education, 20*(2), 147–162.

Berlant, L. G. (2011). *Cruel optimism.* Durham, NC: Duke University Press.

Cvetkovich, A. (2012). *Depression: A public feeling.* Durham, NC: Duke University Press.

Garland-Thomson, R. (2017). *Extraordinary bodies: Figuring physical disability in American culture and literature.* New York, NY: Columbia University Press.

Naraian, S., & Schlessinger, S. (2017). When theory meets the "reality of reality": Reviewing the sufficiency of the social model of disability as a foundation for teacher preparation for inclusive education. *Teacher Education Quarterly, 44*(1), 81–100.

Probyn, E. (2005). *Blush: Faces of shame.* Minneapolis, MN: University of Minnesota Press.

Schlessinger, S. L. (2018). Reclaiming teacher intellectualism through and for inclusive education. *International Journal of Inclusive Education, 22*(3), 268–284.

Seigworth, G. J., & Gregg, M. (2010). An inventory of shimmers. In M. Gregg, G. J. Seigworth & S. Ahmed (Eds.), *The affect theory reader* (pp. 1–28). Durham, NC: Duke University Press.

Chapter 3

Recognizing Success, Deferring Competence

With Peter Reitzfeld

"For me, it was important to recognize the successes, where things went well, what I accomplished either day to day or at the end of the year. Looking back on it, looking at everything, trying to look at things objectively and looking at what was successful, what worked."

Peter stood out among his peers not just because, as he reminded his own students, his head was colder than their own (it was fully shaven), but also because he had a different set of life experiences than his peers. A father of two and married to a teacher, Peter was in his forties and had enrolled in this program after many years as a professional freelance photographer. Soon after graduation from the program, Peter took up a position as a special educator in a school where he led a self-contained "bridge" class of sixth, seventh and eighth grade students in Humanities. He also co-taught (as the special educator) in a collaboratively taught eighth grade humanities class with another general educator, as well as a collaboratively taught eighth grade math class. At the start of the year, he felt comfortable that he had made the right decision in selecting this school. He felt mostly able to enact his commitments, even though he did not always agree with the decisions taken by the administration.

By the end of that year, Peter had decided to move to a different school where he had completed his student teaching experience and where one of his cohort members was already working. His decision to leave was prompted mostly by the desire to be mentored into becoming more effective as a teacher. He could therefore acknowledge significant gains he had made over a tumultuous first year; however, he also recognized the necessity to develop his own skills. His co-teacher in the new location was also a mentor from his student teaching year; he looked forward to the higher expectations that would be placed on him in the coming year, "because there's no more, you know, bullshit, fires or rocks to hide behind."

This "bullshit, fires or rocks" that he continually dodged during his first year nevertheless occasioned much reflection on his self-competence and his burgeoning identity as an educator. Coming out of the program, he, like the other members of his cohort, welcomed the radical constructivism offered by the program on inclusion; he actively took up a stance towards learning as always interwoven with contextual factors and as situated within deeply flawed schooling structures. Yet, from the start, his positions were inevitably accompanied by a persistent recognition of a material "reality" that demanded consideration when teaching. We characterize Peter's first year experience as realist-constructivist; we see him as continually, if unevenly, holding on to both visions of teaching/learning, despite the inevitable dilemmas this created for him.

Looking Forward ... to Experience!

Competence as a teacher, for Peter, was neither easily defined nor was it readily recognizable. Yet, in assessing such competence, he argued for a kinder, gentler self-evaluative stance, given that he and his peers lacked "experience." As first year teachers, he and the members of his cohort were required to be uncertain and anxious—only experience, which they could not possibly *have* at this time, could afford them the answers they craved. Understanding experience in this sense, as a property within an individual that provides access to knowledge, afforded some benefits. So, the best evaluative response to oneself at this time was to be generous to oneself. He observed: "I mean do I want an *Ineffective*? Absolutely not. But am I OK with *Developing*? F—k, yeah, this is my first year. I'm not even, you know, halfway through my first year. So, I'm *Developing*." The forward-looking focus on *developing experience*, rather than *claiming* some special *knowledge* allowed him to recognize his growth in the midst of a first year of teaching marked by persistent student disengagement, unreliable co-teachers, curricular uncertainties and struggles with classroom discipline. Particularly in regard to student engagement, he recognized his struggle as shared with other veteran teachers and that was "part of the reason why I don't go home and cry every night." He understood that when one was "in it," it was difficult to discern the growth and the successes one had achieved. At the end of the year, then, taking stock of all that happened, he could assert confidently that he had done

> a lot more learning and growing than I think I realized. I just know that I'm going to look back next year and be able to draw from my experiences of last year in ways that I don't think I'm appreciating or aware of right now.

In Peter's emergent sense of himself as an educator, competence was a *deferred* attribute dependent not only on the benefits of time, but to the infinite and unpredictable teaching/learning encounters produced via the passage of time and, presumably, across spaces. Competence, in his view, seemed to be the collective *mining* of those encounters—a process that was itself unconstrained by place or time. As Peter *mined* the experiences of his first year with us, he disclosed the complexity of coming to understand inclusive teaching.

Just "Good Teaching"

During group conversations and interviews, Peter returned frequently to the idea that the complexity of the work in which the group was engaged was less about special education or inclusive education, but about "good teaching." In doing so, he was not necessarily affirming the institution of special education; on the contrary, he was suggesting that the inclusive philosophy learned within his special education program was "more humanistic" than "typical general educators' programs." Such a humanistic orientation would benefit all students. In that regard, he visualized a time in the future when there would be no need for special or general educators. Special education would be "outdated" and he and his peers would all be "just good teachers."

Peter's vision of "good teaching" was grounded in the notion of creating accessibility for all. Noting the idea that, "Not everybody can use stairs, but everybody can use a ramp" he expected that all students, including those marginalized by race, ability, class, could be folded into a "good teaching" approach that would afford each student the opportunity and means to learn. It was this that allowed him to make student engagement fundamental to his philosophy of education. Not surprisingly, during his first year, it was the *dis*engagement of his students that preoccupied him and which repeatedly surfaced in his struggles. He grappled continually with curricular and pedagogical ways to arouse student interest so that they could show greater engagement.

Peter carried forward this belief in "good teaching" in other dimensions of his practice, particularly in the ways he conceptualized the division between general and special education. Despite the clear distinctions made between general and special education in his school, his assigned role of a special educator did not prevent him from trying to bridge that divide. In the classroom where he taught collaboratively with a general educator, he actively discounted such divisions and worked just as much with non-disabled students as he did with students with documented disabilities. Peter clearly felt competent to provide instructional support to all students.

Researchers have wondered if notions of "good teaching" can encompass the particular difference that disability makes (Michalko, 2001). In other words, can "good teaching" automatically perform a resistance to, or a dismantling of the ableist infrastructure of schooling? Peter's "just good teaching" practice, as we learn in the next section, evidenced a complex orientation; it drew on his persistent awareness of a range of material and social factors implicated within the phenomenon of disability and implicitly raises the question of how resistance to ableist practices can itself be recognized.

Reconciling "Real" and "Constructed"

During this first year, Peter struggled continually to reconcile "real" and "constructed" perspectives, particularly as related to student performance. From the beginning of *our* own relations with Peter during his graduate program of study, we understood him as willing to accept the concept of disability as a socially constructed phenomenon, but not quite ready to abandon an acknowledgement of the embodied reality of learning difference. Indeed, his words provoked the title for our article describing the learning of this cohort (Naraian & Schlessinger, 2017). Peter might well be articulating what many post-positivist realists have stated, that is, that a phenomenon (in this case, disability) may be socially constructed, but is not *only* socially constructed (Moya, 2000).

Not surprisingly, disability within Peter's view, was simultaneously real and acquired. In his words:

> We are getting students who have suffered from lack of socioeconomic resources at home at critical points of their learning and development [such] that what may have not been a learning disability has perpetuated itself into a learning disability. And I don't know how much of that is based on their previous history and experience at home and in school.

This attunement to materiality may well have fueled Peter's argument for the necessity for medication in some cases to address some learning struggles, even as it evoked uncertainty about others, such as student behavioral challenges. In the latter case, he confessed: "I don't know how much of that is real learning struggles and how much of that is just putting out fires." As he confronted a seemingly unending presentation of such behavioral challenges in his everyday instructional practice, he wondered whether it might result from an obstinate refusal to capitulate to school expectations. He was suspicious, therefore, of the process by which students were labeled. His comments in a paper written during his preparatory year disclosed the continuity in his perspective on this issue. Describing a student in his student teaching placement, Peter had argued: "I do believe that learning disability is a legitimate category of disability; however, I believe its diagnosis should be judiciously doled out: currently, it is not." He continued to maintain this recognition of disability as "real" during his initial year of teaching. Yet, Peter was clearly aware of the effects of societal inequities on student lives that could produce "disability," as well as the flawed processes of schooling that resulted in a faulty implementation of a concept intended to be helpful.

Peter's simultaneous recognition of embodied realities and social processes delivered dilemmas in the school/classroom some of which he was able to resolve satisfactorily, while others left him more uncertain. While he would gladly agree with his students that removing their hats was "a stupid rule," he still did not dismiss the utility of following some norms, such as being on time, and not "just rolling in when they [saw] fit." In other words, Peter could see some norms as capable of constructing students as failures. His intervention was to modulate the impact of such norms by extending some recognition of the students' embodied needs; therefore, he felt comfortable making some adjustments to routine procedures and rules. For instance, he was able to negotiate with a particular student about listening to music in the classroom to help his concentration, as long as that adjustment helped that student to be productive in the classroom. Or, he might be able to ensure that the learning supports needed by a student were in place even if the school was technically unable to provide a collaboratively taught classroom as documented on his IEP. Each individual instance carried a potential threat to Peter; either to his competence as a teacher who could produce successful learners or to his standing as a teacher of record discharging his legal responsibilities. In each, Peter was aware of the boundaries he was skirting, but felt confident to take the risks entailed in each.

Such boundaries were much harder to identify and negotiate when he was confronted with repeated instances of collective student noncompliance or disengagement. He upheld the significance of building relationships as key to student learning, and therefore as partially constructing student success. However, a socially constructed view of student learning that called for such responsive instructional practice could not always be sustained. Frustrated by the chronic disengagement of students in his classrooms and the ineffectiveness of the curricular measures he undertook to raise their motivation for academic work, he fell back on using external consequences to enforce expectations of desired behaviors. This might mean using detentions as a deterrent, changing classroom seating assignments, or offering reduced assignments to encourage students to aspire for a passing grade. Such external measures brought some, if limited, success.

Throughout his first year, he grappled with the unpredictable effects of his pedagogical moves to elicit student engagement. His forays into a more "realist" approach notwithstanding, (or perhaps *because* of that) we see Peter as still securely ensconced in a social constructionist zone. He learned to re-negotiate his relationships with the students; he came to see the benefits of accepting his students without judgment. He found that "letting go of his expectations" did not mean abandoning high standards for his students; rather it forced him to ask himself: "What expectations can I let go of in the hopes of accomplishing more and creating a better community or a better environment?" He sought to treat his students "differently than they were used to being treated" taking as many opportunities as possible to affirm to his students that he recognized them as persons with unique gifts and strengths.

Performativity Versus Authenticity: "Playing the Game of School"

Implicit in Peter's stories was the premise that school needed to be partly understood as a game. As he wisely noted, the rules of school required certain performances. He recognized that some students could and did play the game of school, but others could not. He distinguished students in his self-contained class who "were there to be students; there, to play the game of school" from those in other classrooms who "just don't care" and were not there to "be students." Peter's metaphor of school as a game surfaces matters of authenticity and performance for students and teachers alike. Performances veer away from authenticity; schooling, by its very nature then, could not guarantee authenticity. The struggle for both Peter (and possibly, his students) may have been to find as many spaces and opportunities as possible to surface authentic expressions.

Peter's understanding of his own teaching as a performance may also have derived in part from the unreliability of student participation. He described with much joy and animation when, on one occasion students embraced his prepared lesson on Taoism; as he walked around "slapping hands" relishing the ways they were participating actively, it felt like "a real beautiful moment of our community functioning at its height." Yet, he also knew that a lesson the following day might evoke just the very opposite; students disengaged and refusing to "be students." His confusion was sincere as he asked himself, "what did I do that day that was able to bring everybody in. And what, or what did I do on other days that doesn't bring everybody in?" Students, too, it seemed, might be performing, though not always in expected ways. He was aware that students could perform for others' benefit; it mattered to them that they be understood as capable by others, particularly the administration.

When Peter characterized his students as "play[ing] their role" in the school he clearly saw himself as part of their performance, too. For instance, on the occasion when he was being observed by the administrators, it happened that the students' performance was enthusiastic and animated. Even though he felt competent in this situation, he remarked that "it was kind of playing school." Peter recognized the performative nature of schooling where one became primed to "know who's watching when;" such recognition reflects the complex social dynamics in a school context that are governed by multiple rules of interaction across different spaces within the building. Peter's struggle for authenticity is best explained by him: "I don't feel like I'm *not* being true to myself, because I feel like I'm always honest and transparent with the students; but I do feel a little bit more that I'm playing that game in terms of 'this is what we're supposed to be doing.'" The mandated compliance to certain social norms whether one agreed with them or not, constrained everyone's performance including his own. His claim to authenticity was to continually push the boundaries of those norms, whether it was by bending the rules of eating food in class or good-humoredly refusing to call students out on inappropriate language use.

Teaching-learning as a "game" required coming to know and understand the art and craft of one's own enactment (including curricular ones) in relation to others. It should be more than "putting out" fires and in that regard, his first year did not help him develop knowledge of the craft of teaching. There was no uniform curriculum in the school and Peter discovered that each teacher developed their own curriculum. Even if he had good ideas for curricular content, "in terms of actually putting it together and piecing together resources and materials and then developing them," he felt woefully inadequate. His lack of fluency in content areas exacerbated by the absence of a given curriculum made him feel like a "fake." His own need to work slowly on gathering materials furthered this anxiety.

Peter's understanding of teaching-learning as a game, then, may well have reflected his own search for authenticity. This surfaced particularly in the ways he described his successes. Rather than curricular or pedagogical, the accomplishments he identified were relational; he reported making "good connections" with both students and colleagues. "That is something that is clear to me. It's that with a room full of students I can be authentic, and it can be received in such a way that it's legitimate. It's real." In the performative acts in which both teachers and students were engaged, it was the moments of authenticity he shared with his students that conferred a "real-ness" to the experience of teaching. Indeed, it was this "authenticity" that he felt also endeared him to his colleagues who respected his "genuine" interactions with everyone. Such moments notwithstanding, the desire to hone the craft of teaching drove him to seek a position at a different school.

The above interpretive reading of Peter as primary agent within his narrative disclosed his struggles with students and curriculum, his evolving interpretation of his role as teacher and his optimistic stance towards his own competence. It placed full emphasis on Peter's capability to enact inclusive teaching commitments, that is, it asked: to what extent is Peter able to carry out the goals of inclusive education? What if we focused instead on the *enactment* of inclusion via Peter (and also other entities), rather than on Peter's *capability* to do so? In other words, how does inclusive teaching get produced via Peter? What more might a focus on *the performative aspect of inclusive teaching* rather than on *individual* (Peter's) *sense-making*, as we have done thus far, tell us about novice inclusive teaching? Could we learn something about the relations between the different elements that collectively produce enactments of teaching and learning? Said differently, if we did not presume that Peter alone was responsible for his inclusive education performances, what else might we learn?

In the following pages, we continue to explore Peter's story, through a *diffractive* methodology (Barad, 2007) that looks for overlaps and interferences between different bodies and objects that produce the phenomena of novice inclusive teaching.

Continuing to Understand Peter's Becoming: Reading Peter "diffractively"

"The idea of trying to be a teacher in this environment is very difficult."

In narrating Peter diffractively, we are, counterintuitively, first required to focus on the phenomenon of "inclusion" or "inclusive teaching" rather than on the intentionality of a single agent, in this case Peter (Barad, 2008). Drawing on Barad's notion of *agential realism* that posits that "agents" are both human and non-human, material and cultural/ discursive, we can go further and consider "inclusion" as entailing an arrangement or assemblage of people, practices and ideas. All such "bodies" and "objects" are both materially *and* discursively formed. This allows us to offer a materially grounded understanding of Peter's teaching for inclusion; we could see Peter as engaged in *intra-activity* with many material-discursive elements as he carries out his enactment of inclusive teaching. Additionally, we realize that we, as researchers, are also entangled in the ways we come to understand Peter's year as a novice teacher. The themes we have described in the previous section emerged from a particular "apparatus of knowing" (Taguchi & Palmer, 2013) that *we* employed as researchers and interpreters of Peter. For instance, within the theories we brought to understand Peter's experience, an inclusive teacher always presumes the competence (Biklen & Burke, 2006) of his/her students, and monitors and interrogates rules of school (normative conceptions of teaching/learning). Peter, too, we might argue, enacted his inclusive teacher-*ness* from within this *frame of knowing.*

We wondered if locating Peter in intra-action with other material-discursive "agents" such as students, rules of school, discourses of competence/success, administration, and co-teachers, may deepen our understanding of Peter's *becoming* as an inclusive educator.[1] We understood Peter's inclusive teacher-*ness* as entangled with the becoming of these and other "agents". In the following pages, we explore the relations between some "agents" entangled within Peter's enactments of an inclusive teacher to understand his *becoming* more deeply. We focus on rules of school and teacher competence to surface these linkages.

Rules of School

The rules of school, as indicated in the previous section, referred to the normative expectations of school/classroom performance that included expectations of timely arrival, of participation in classroom processes, of responsiveness to teachers' directions and initiations, and of aspiring for school success. Peter's relations with these rules was mandatory—he was after all, a teacher charged with upholding responsibilities towards students in this school. These relations produced multiple effects. It led to Peter's frustration with students whose disregard for such rules made them (the students) seem incomprehensible and unpredictable. "I can't figure out what would make a student with an 85 decide not to hand this in other than they didn't value it for whatever reason that might be." Yet, Peter also recognized the arbitrariness of these school-wide expectations and in his willingness to continually negotiate their enforcement with students, these rules emerged as *elastic* and *malleable,* though still necessary for student success. Efforts towards inclusion, we might infer, may materialize differently depending on the ways school norms are allowed to be continually stretched and/or made elastic. At the same time, students' apparent disregard for the rules of school which Peter was obliged to uphold, were at least partially responsible for the uncertainty that informed Peter's teaching.

Peter recognized the cultural-historical and socioeconomic origins of student disengagement from the rules of school, but he was simultaneously entangled with school-wide teacher discourses of student (in)competence and failure. This, not surprisingly, injected tension within his enactments of inclusion. In one instance, Peter spoke about introducing a new curricular topic following a school-wide testing event, with the intention of placing minimal cognitive demands on them, fully aware that these eighth grade students might be resistant to classroom work on a day of "testing." Since they were in the midst of learning about Civil Rights and change during the 20th century, he introduced some clips of speeches by Malcolm X to distinguish it from the perspective brought by Martin Luther King. He reasoned that by not including a writing exercise, there would not be a significant cognitive load on students.

> We're just going to talk. We're going to listen to this man talk and say some very different stuff … and they wouldn't have it. So, I tried to persevere through it. And at the end, I said: OK. So, it's obvious this isn't interesting to you. What would you guys like to do? And they said: Watch a movie. I said: OK. What kind of movie? And they said: Anything from Netflix. I said: So, an entertainment movie. And they said: Yeah. And I said: And why? And they said: 'Cause, we took a test today. I said: So, you sat for an hour and a half test and that warrants the whole rest of the day off for three days. And they said: Yeah. So I said: OK.

Peter's account of the event discloses the tension that coexisted with enacting a compassionate inclusive teacher to his students alongside the rules of school. It produced students both as unreasonable and yet, capable of rational behavior. It simultaneously disclosed his own ambivalent stance towards such norms—should school rules always be followed? He revealed himself as an educator deeply attached to the desire to stimulate student interest/engagement, as willing to negotiate, and eventually, as willing to yield to them. He continued: "So the next day, I brought in the movie *Malcolm X*. Cause I figured, why not try …? And they were just like: 'Spike Lee sucks. There's no way.'" Producing little positive effect, his approach to serving curriculum while supportive of students' desires eventually had to be abandoned.

Peter mused:

> I think I'm going to kind of just let go these next three days where we have the math test and just kind of, just go with that and try to give them what they

want even though in my heart of hearts I don't really feel they deserve it. As much as I love them.

Peter's embodied understanding of himself as an inclusive teacher required loving relationships with students, to "treat them differently than they are used to," but this could only be made possible by a continual shifting of his own relations with the rules of school and school-wide discourses on student competence. Such a process might mark his students as "undeserving" on some occasions. However, during other times, as in his decision to massage the rules, he demonstrated an understanding of students as needing to be affirmed rather than alienated from school. In other words, student behavior did not mean that *they* were willful or manipulative nor did it suggest that Peter was ineffective. Rather, *their* (dis)engagement came to matter alongside *Peter's* own relations with school-wide norms of student behavior. Student engagement and Peter's own competence were entangled within a process marked by fluidity and change.

Teacher Competence

Relations with students were consequential. Peter's sense of competence as an inclusive teacher remained continually vulnerable to the capability of those relationships to produce student learning performance as measured by the rules of school. Student participation in classroom curricular activity "made [him] feel competent" just as the absence of it evoked deep anxiety in him: "I'm trying to accomplish something, but this is not working. And what am I not doing ...?" Peter identified the origins of his anxiety about curricular competence as residing partly in his lack of fluency in content area knowledge (for e.g., math and history), and the lack of time at his disposal to develop curricular resources, even though he felt confident about his ideas. But his decision-making on curriculum inevitably bumped up against the rules of School. If it was acceptable, for instance, to use the music of popular artists like Jay-Z to hook students into a lesson, he worried about how exactly the connections to the topic at hand should be made? In other words, the rules of school also required him to monitor the types of curricular content that might be permissible in a middle school classroom.

Interestingly, the co-evolution of his practice, student learning and school discourses of competence, marked the passage of time in specific ways. Peter's recognition by the end of the academic year of the significance of "letting go of the expectations" that is, not holding students up against the rules of school, but instead to "accept" them for who they were or to "combine [expectations] with love and support," allowed him to describe his first year as one when he "did a lot of growing." This sense of time materialized alongside his recognition of his own competence: "I learned that what I bring to the table is significant and substantial in a way that maybe I didn't appreciate before." As his relationships with his students improved, it evoked a growing confidence in his capacity as a teacher. Such confidence in the present moment was simultaneously large enough to acknowledge his present *in*capacity as temporary, because greater success is now deferred to the future—"I also know that I have a lot more growing to do."

Peter's account registers the *temporal* nature of competence; it is evoked within the present moment via past material-discursive activity—Peter's enactments of inclusive teaching with and alongside students and the rules of school—and as continually deferred to an open-ended future. As novice educators then, it would be impossible to experience competence; it was always already projected into the future. Yet, counterintuitively, *success* could still be investigated in the present through a deliberate overturning of this temporal structure. Peter illustrates this when he offers this question as a means to evaluate his achievement: "What did you accomplish compared to what has been or what could have been?" This form of looking back to a conditional past to anticipate a different future could afford an understanding of success in the present moment that was very different, yet very "valuable."

Reading into Both Accounts

Peter's immersion in the game of school disclosed the oppressive effects of school norms that are both explicit and lie below the surface. By using an approach to his narrative that understood Peter as always entangled with other elements, we learn that the important task assigned to inclusive educators of identifying and disrupting norms may be more intricate and complicated than may be immediately apparent. It calls for a recognition that such norms are ubiquitous in the everyday enactments of teaching and learning. Any investigation of such norms requires materially grounded analyses. It renders Peter's quest for the "real" as the ground on which efforts towards inclusion must be predicated, wherein such "reality" refers to what elements *come to matter,* and how. Peter's entanglements of practice may be vastly different in another, no less "real" site of inclusion.

A materially informed understanding of inclusion, then requires an awareness of the entanglements that collectively evoke inclusion. Indeed, such awareness can complicate individualized notions of *competencies* that novice educators are supposed to have acquired at the end of their preparation and before they enter the field. Our understanding of Peter's narrative discloses that competencies may be loosened from within the body of the educator; we may instead understand them as relational and as materializing differently within different school contexts.

Peter: Five Years Later

Teaching is a complex profession. The levels of what is required logistically and pedagogically on a daily basis are numerous and can often overshadow the element at the heart of the job: we work with kids. These are human beings with individual and complex needs, backgrounds, social interactions and family dynamics; additionally, we do this work during a formative time of their lives.

Many teachers enter the profession citing a life-long calling or childhood desire. I did not. A career-changer, I came to teaching as an adult with two children of my own, and the life experience to know things don't always go the way they "should," or how you hope or plan. This understanding played a role in my pre-service training as well as in my first year in the classroom. Being an inclusive special educator in the NYC public school system, the relationship between the theoretical and reality often don't line up. My first school and first year of teaching presented challenges extending beyond the typical learning curve of starting a new occupation, but perhaps not so unique to other first-year teachers. Having an intense program consisting of two subject areas, three curriculums (two of which were not provided) and students spanning three grade levels, with a diverse range of academic/socio-emotional needs and (dis)abilities does not set a new teacher up for feeling successful.

My stance on education and learning remains grounded in a belief of the importance of authentic relationships and intrinsic motivation. I maintain now, as I did during my pre-service training, that kids see through facades and that nothing is as valuable to a child's education as their own interest-generated engagement. However, reality provides a major stumbling block to this well-intentioned position. As a first-year teacher, it was not that the real-life stressors in my students' lives were not foreseen or unanticipated, it is more how truly deep they cut. The issues many of my students faced outside the classroom were severe enough to trivialize what was going on inside the classroom in a manner that challenged the implementation of theoretical strategies and ideas. It is difficult for a 13-year-old to engage with solving a two-step equation when his mother did not come home for the second or third night in a row. How can that child play the role of student—valuing what is going on in a math classroom—when he thinks this may be the beginning of another month-long absence of his mother, whether he will be left in the care of his 19-year-old sister—a child likely brought up in the same unstable environment, likely facing the same socio-emotional needs? How can a teacher, especially one with little experience, hope to prove that he or she is there for that child in a meaningful way to build a relationship, and expect to engage them with an academic curriculum? These are challenges that only experience can prepare one to even try and attempt to take on.

Beyond the vast socio-emotional/economic needs of our students in our schools, there is a diverse range of abilities. From students ready and eager to take on curricular material several years above their current grade level, to students who have difficulty correctly identifying shapes. Students with IEPs (Individual Education Programs) are labeled with a disability, for which they receive Special Education services. Within this group of students labeled with disabilities there is variety as well. There are those with constructed disabilities, learned (or manifested) disabilities, and those who experience legitimate barriers to learning, processing and understanding. Again, it is through personal experience with these students that one can to navigate—or even try to understand—the differences between these "disabilities," and how to work with these children.

One's first year, tasked with learning and implementing all the logistical and pedagogical aspects of the job is challenging enough on its own. Combining this with the emotional, human-connection facet at the root of the profession, made feeling successful elusive for this self-reflective career-changer with self-imposed high standards and expectations. My first year of teaching was one of immersion. It is difficult to name the levels of complexity we must deal with on a daily basis. The rigors of the job, day-to-day are clear: planning lessons, designing and creating material, culling resources, assessing students' work and progress, writing IEPs etc., these are taxing in their own way, which is to be expected. The unexpected, or should I say, underexpected piece is the emotionally fatiguing aspect of the job. This has to do with one's self-imposed expectations, of course, but also to what extent one takes on, or fits into, the stories of their students. As an empathetic person (as I would wager most who go into this profession are) this is difficult to manage, especially combined with the other realities and requirements, but it is particularly amplified during the first year. During that period, I had difficulty seeing the growth in my students and myself. It is the perspective of time and the experience of that year that granted me the feeling of accomplishment and success, which was difficult to own while immersed in the experience. Going forward I have learned to identify small gains and to recognize them as wins. I have learned to value progress not perfection, and give myself the freedom to try, fail, and try again—exactly what we ask of our students.

Note

1 We capitalize these entities to denote each as an agent; within new materialist approaches, each agent affects and is affected by others.

References

Barad, K. (2007). *Meeting the universe halfway: Quantum physics and the entanglement of matter and meaning.* Durham, NC: Duke University Press.

Barad, K. (2008). Posthumanist performativity: Toward an understanding of how matter comes to matter. In S. Alaimo & S. Hekman (Eds.), *Material feminisms* (pp. 120–154). Bloomington, IN: Indiana University Press.

Biklen, D., & Burke, J. (2006). Presuming competence. *Equity & Excellence in Education, 39*, 166–175.

Michalko, R. (2001). *The difference that disability makes.* Philadelphia: Temple University Press.

Moya, P. M. L. (2000). Post-modernism, "realism," and the politics of identity: Cherrie Moraga and Chicana feminism. In P. M. L. Moya & M. R. Hames-Garcia (Eds.), *Reclaiming identity: Realist theory and the predicament of postmodernism* (pp. 67–101). Berkeley, CA: University of California Press.

Naraian, S., & Schlessinger, S. (2017). When theory meets the "reality of reality": Reviewing the sufficiency of the social model of disability as a foundation for teacher preparation for inclusive education. *Teacher Education Quarterly, 44*(1), 81-100.

Taguchi, H. L., & Palmer, A. (2013). A more "livable" school? A diffractive analysis of the performative enactments of girls' ill-/well-being with(in) school environments. *Gender and Education, 25*(6), 671–687.

Chapter 4

Stories of a Feminist Killjoy Inclusive Educator

With Harley Jones

"I'm always so aware of when people have more experience than I do. And I think I tend to defer to that."

In many ways, Harley's experience as a first-year teacher can be characterized by her experience of, and attachment to, being "expert." Harley came to her graduate education having worked in charter schools and as a paraprofessional. In her cohort of MA students, Harley was often positioned by her peers as the "expert" on "the way it is" in schools, a positioning she took up readily. In our group conversations about theoretical critiques of the system and idealistic possibilities, Harley could answer the practical questions that her classmates had about schooling. And these answers were derived from and delivered with a confidence in her own knowledge and understanding of a system and profession in which she had more experience than any of her peers. Yet, as Harley moved from former paraprofessional, to graduate student, and into teacher, this confidence in her "expertise" seemed to waiver. Increasingly, she began to see herself as the less experienced, less knowledgeable, and less expert pedagogue in the classroom and to question her own conceptualization of professionalism and pedagogical practice, despite her specifically necessary role as the special/inclusive educator in the room.

In this chapter, working from an affective lens, we offer an investigation into the ways that Harley took up (or not) her role in her classroom as a colleague, instructional leader, and inclusive teacher, as well as into her teacher-student relationships that were mediated by her identity as a white, female, inclusive educator. Specifically, we draw on Harley's own invocations of gender dynamics in her school and classroom to explore the ways in which attachments to femininities mediated her "becoming" an inclusive educator in this first year of teaching and her production of inclusion vis-a vis this concept of self.

The Classroom as the Happy Home

During Harley's first year of teaching following her graduate program, she taught in the humanities as the special education counterpart in two co-teaching relationships. Both of her co-teachers were men who had more years of teaching experience than she did. One of them, Thomas had been teaching for 20 years. Harley felt as though she had "known him for a very long time" and that he reminded her "of my great uncles—like my Jewish uncles." Dan, her other co-teacher, had been teaching for four years, and while he and Harley got along, she did not experience the same immediate level of comfort with him as she did with Thomas. The two partnerships provided her different opportunities to explore her own teacher identity and learn about curricular design and enactment, but at the end of the day, Harley felt that "as much as I think it can be an amazing thing to have two teachers in a classroom, I can't shake the feeling of 'But really, I want my own class.'" In both contexts, Harley struggled to find her own sense of "expertise" and her role as the special educator, sharing that "there have been times where I felt like, 'Oh, I'm in the corner and he's like star of the show' and it's not a great feeling."

In part because of this not-great feeling and also because Harley consistently reflected on her own actions and experiences, she spent a significant amount of time and emotional energy trying to make sense of these co-teaching relationships; they mattered to her sense of self and her development as teacher. Despite her previous experience in schools and her completion of her master's degree in inclusive secondary education, she understood herself as novice in this role and context especially in comparison with her co-teachers. She had learned through her graduate studies that the role of special educator could sometimes be murky. Friend and Cook (1992) have defined co-teaching as the shared planning for and instruction of all students in a classroom by two teachers using six different structures for collaboration. Unfortunately, co-teaching is often enacted as a general education teacher designing the curriculum, writing the lessons, leading instruction, and asking for a special educator to make modifications that will support students with disabilities (Pugach & Winn, 2011). This was Harley's experience. She knew that as the special educator she could have more of a role in the planning and teaching in her classrooms, but she was primarily asked to play a support role to her co-teachers. Even as she recognized these somewhat problematic positionings of her as novice and as special educator, Harley still felt that power dynamics in her co-teaching relationships were unequal and uncomfortable in a way that could not be fully explained by her limited years of experience or special education certification. She felt that

> some of it (*the power*) is valid and some of it's not. But especially given my own upbringing and gender roles and all of these things and expectations of power and where power is between genders, I definitely still find myself having to remember that I'm as equal of a voice in defining myself as they are.

Her understanding of herself as an educator and her role as the special educator within co-teaching relationships was, she felt, mediated by (among other things) her gender. In the field of special and inclusive education, the co-teaching partnership is often compared to a marriage (Howard & Potts, 2009; Murawski, 2009; Sileo, 2011). Given this framing in the field and Harley's own concern about the gendered ways of being within her co-teaching relationships as she grew into an inclusive teacher, we find it compelling to conceptualize the classroom as "The Happy Household" and draw on Sarah Ahmed's (2010) theorizing around the "happy housewife" and the "feminist killjoy" to consider

Harley's co-teaching experience during this first year of her teaching and "becoming" an inclusive educator.

The Happy Housewife/Happy Special Educator

Harley spoke frequently about her struggles with Dan, and we will return those shortly, but first it seems valuable to dig into the "uncle" relationship with Thomas. Alongside his 20 years of teaching experience, Thomas brought with him "a curriculum that was not set ... but he'd clearly planned very carefully in the past." Through his own "expertise," his previously planned coursework, and his relational (perhaps mentor-like) approach to his co-teaching relationship with Harley, Thomas offered her a comfortable space to, as she put it, "just learn from and see how another teacher, who is experienced, structured his curriculum." In this space, she could follow the expectations of her senior, male counterpart and, in the performance of these expectations, achieve the status of "good" special education teacher. Ahmed (2010) offers that happiness provides a script for the becoming of "happy housewife" or a happy woman to be pleasing in the male sight and to earn male respect. That is to say that following the particular "script" of the happy housewife will in and of itself lead to a desired happiness, and that happiness is in part because the role is pleasing to male counterparts. Thus "happiness provides a script for her (the housewife's) becoming" (Ahmed, 2010, p.55). Harley and Thomas's configuration of the co-teaching partnership took up similar tropes in that Harley's pursuit of happiness as "good" special educator provided a script for her becoming as well. And that script, outlined by Thomas's expertise, planned curriculum, and mentoring, was clearly defined for Harley. Positioning herself via this script as learner and support staff comforted her: she could be a good educator and thereby move towards happiness—happiness for herself and happiness for Thomas, whose perceived expertise positioned him as author of the "happy special educator" script and as the person to please.

Yet, just as Ahmed states that "the happy housewife is a fantasy figure that erases the signs of labor under the sign of happiness," (p.50) so too was this happy special educator a fantasy figure. Performing happy special educator left Harley feeling disempowered, such that even though she liked "the idea of looking just to myself for answers," there was always something that made her "feel like: Oh, I need to ... let me ask (Thomas)." Working with Thomas provided Harley with a script for how to be a good special educator and this script was comforting in its promise of happiness, its promise of success in this role. But in practice, following this script led Harley to a way of being as a teacher that diminished her previous confidence in herself and in her own answers or ideas. She felt herself becoming dependent on Thomas as the expert, which was uncomfortable for her understanding of and desires for herself as an educator. She was aware that following a "happy special educator" script moved her towards Thomas's desires rather than toward her own in a way that made her unhappy, but she was unsure of how to move otherwise.

Harley's "becoming" as inclusive teacher, then, was mediated by the expert/novice co-teaching relationship and the happiness promised through performing good/happy special educator as determined by her senior male counterpart. While it is unclear whether this experience was more impacted by her novice status or by her female positioning and enactment of her femininities, it seems that both intersecting identity markers likely played a role. Not only did this promise of happiness mediate Harley's own becoming, it also mediated her agentive production of inclusion. Following the special educator script and playing a supportive role in the classroom worked as a barrier to redesigning curricula to be more universally accessible and to building culturally responsive entry points into standardized units of study. Instead, she focused "too much" class time on social-emotional supports for students, or in disrupting singular understandings of smartness or success in the classroom. She fell into the role of special educator, differentiating specific lessons that Thomas had planned while supporting individual students. And while there were strengths to this work and successes for her within it, her performance of the happy special educator moved her away from practices of inclusivity that she valued and believed in. Her actualized production of inclusion in this specific space and context shifted away from her commitment to inclusivity learned and developed in graduate school and towards a script for traditional special education supports.

The Emergence of a Feminist Killjoy Troublemaking Inclusive Educator

While Harley's co-teaching relationship with Thomas was comforting to her, her co-teaching relationship with Dan was a significant focus of her frustration and reflection during this year of teacher. Dan, in his fourth year of teaching, certainly occupied a somewhat more experienced role than Harley, but she did not view him with the same fatherly respect as she did Thomas. Consequently, Harley felt both more and less empowered in this co-teaching relationship; more empowered to speak up and assert herself and her ideas as an expert and knowing self, but also more disempowered by the dismissal of these ideas by her co-teacher. Where Thomas offered her comfort that at times felt constraining, Dan and Harley had a somewhat more antagonistic, if still respectful, co-teaching relationship. As the general educator in the room, Dan was considered the lead teacher. In this construction of co-teaching, Dan was, like Thomas, responsible for designing the curriculum and leading the instruction while Harley was responsible for modifying this curriculum to make it accessible to all students and for supporting students who were struggling to engage with the curriculum. This is the dominant enactment of co-teaching in many schools around the nation, including the New York City department of education. Scholars in the fields of special education, critical special education, and disability studies in education have critiqued such practice. Harley had studied and committed to a more a collaborative shared planning and instructional approach to co-teaching.

Upon entering into this classroom, Harley took up her role as curricular modifier and student supporter, much in the same way that she did in her work with Thomas. However, Dan, unlike Thomas, did not have a well-planned "set" curriculum. This context pushed Harley to step out of what her "scripted" role as good special educator was and move toward "being comfortable interrupting someone. You know, like when there are two adults in the room who like to talk, but one of them has been doing it longer … I have to interrupt often." In stepping outside of this scripted role, in interrupting as the special educator instead of hanging back and waiting, Harley was resisting the following of the script and moving away from the promise of happiness that it held. Ahmed (2010) offers that "in order to get along, you have to participate in certain forms of solidarity: you have to laugh at the right points" (p.65). By choosing to not "laugh at the right points" to not sit back and wait her turn, but rather to interrupt and "interrupt often," Harley was acting as what Ahmed would call a "troublemaker" whose "failure to be happy is read as sabotaging the happiness of others"(Ahmed, 2010, p.66). Harley worked hard to make sure that as she interrupted her colleague she did so in careful, even happy, ways "so that the person is not taking it as an affront, but rather like 'oh you missed something.'" For example, much of the language used to talk to and about students in Harley's school and classroom was derived from a deficit model that did not align with Harley's own understanding of disability studies in education, special education or her idealized self as an educator. Rather than directly interrupting Dan's language or pedagogy, Harley felt that:

> if you come at it from the angle of this is the language I want to speak and the only language I want to speak, then it's really problematic. But if you come at it from a way of just, privately, this is what you [as an inclusive educator] know and understand, and then enact it in ways that make sense in that environment, it's awesome.

This self-restraint on speech and deliberate focus on enactment was a strategy that Harley used to increase her presence in the classroom. In this way, she acted to disrupt the happy special educator script without offending her co-teacher.

Despite her efforts to be a palatable troublemaker, Harley's relationship with Dan was fraught with tension, which she located in its intensity and its gendered dynamics. Harley felt that she and Dan respected each other as colleagues, but she expressed feeling somewhat overwhelmed by their relationship. She was frustrated by spending so much time with a person (Dan) "that it just makes you connect with them even when you don't necessarily feel like it. It [the time] sort of forces you into it." In order to keep the peace, to not be "read as sabotaging the happiness"(Ahmed, 2010) of her co-teacher, Harley allowed for an intensity of a relationship where Dan seemed to position himself as her "protector" or "the person who chooses for me what's OK and what's good and what I should do and what I shouldn't do ... like the patriarchy or something." Acting as a troublemaker in their happy household of a classroom positioned Harley as a "feminist killjoy," which created discomfort for Dan and contingently for her. This discomfort opened space in their relationship for the imposition of a patriarchal script wherein Dan was the caretaker and Harley could once again play the Happy Housewife. It was not until Harley stopped trying to soften her classroom interruptions and her special educator *troublemaking*, not until she directly confronted Dan about his behavior "approaching a boundary that (she) didn't like" that she was able to claim her space in her classroom and the role that she wanted to play. She shared that "that was the most direct we've been around that type of thing. Typically, I kind of joke it off or, you know, let it go." But after that confrontation, she "felt much more comfortable stepping up. I'm just going to do this part as opposed to needing to wait for him to be like: 'Here's this part that I made for you. Or here's this part that you could, if you want.'"

As Harley moved toward and away from following a special educator script, acting as a teaching support in the classroom rather than a teacher, she experienced herself as a not-so happy "happy housewife"/ special educator and/or as a feminist killjoy "troublemaking" inclusive educator. These affective scripts of success, competence, and compliance as a special educator mediated Harley's figuring of her own teacher identity and teacher competency producing feelings of success, comfort, challenge and frustration. These conflicting emotions worked on her practice as an inclusive educator in her classroom. Her decisions to enact inclusivity were more often than not driven by these feelings just as much as (if not more than) by her knowledge of inclusive practice or her commitment to inclusion.

Coming to Care as a Feminist Killjoy Professional Inclusive Educator

Alongside this relational work with her co-teachers that engaged a large part of Harley's first year of teaching, she also grappled with similarly complex relational work with her students. Grounded in her previous classroom and professional experiences, Harley had developed her own understanding of her role in "a professional environment where (she was) providing a service," that required a level of distance between herself and the students receiving her services. Although Harley's coursework had specifically addressed the significance of relational work with students as foundational for inclusion, she was very conscious of being initially drawn towards *de*personalized relationships with her students. She shared that when she began teaching, she had "this expectation ... that I should be able to turn a switch on where I am a professional and I am not so sidetracked by a student who's acting a little weird." Having previously measured her ability to be professional by her ability to put aside possible social and emotional needs of her students and prioritize academic learning, Harley struggled with the line between being "professional" and being "caring" as she developed her understandings of herself as an inclusive educator.

Professionalism is a complicated term in the field of education. While it is a key competency in most teacher education programs, there are vague understandings, at best, of what is meant by professionalism. Creasy (2015) has defined professional teacher behaviors as "observable actions that demonstrate the individual's appropriate behaviors such as: maintaining appropriate relationships with students, parents, and colleagues," (p.24). The word "appropriate" here is still highly relative and contingent on one's theory of teaching and learning. Murray (2006) describes a "double bind" for female educators wherein common-place understandings of professionalism privilege so-called male "rational" ways of being (such as assertiveness), while diminishing the importance of so-called female "emotional" ways of being (such as caretaking). At the same time, teaching and learning are deeply personal activities premised on relational and emotional experiences. Murray (2006) suggests that in teaching, "a significant proportion of this activity is undertaken by women for whom it is a fundamental and unacknowledged part of their work" (p.391). Put simply, it may be unprofessional but necessary to be engaged in caring relationships with students.

Harley's desire to be respected as an expert and taken seriously by her colleagues and her students, combined with her previous experience in the classroom, led her to believe that the femininity of demonstrating care, or at least too much care, was a weakness. She commented: "I want them to like me. And I want to like them. However, sometimes as a first year teacher, that can be to the detriment of getting something done or pushing a student in a way that they are definitely needing to be pushed." She was concerned that relating to and with her students would impede her capacity to teach them, hold them accountable for their work, and hold them to high standards. She had seen both of her "co-teachers do it to great effect where there's a difference between being mean and being challenging." She could acknowledge that teachers did not have to have bad or aggressive relationships with their students in order to hold the students accountable to high standards. Nevertheless, she did not feel that demonstrating care and love would allow her to do the same. Nel Noddings (2015) has written at length about pedagogies of caring and the complexities of working from a pedagogy of caring in a society and school system that is designed around white male privilege. She writes that "for centuries women were expected to seek connection—indeed to put marriage and stable human relations above all else" and "to hide their intelligence" (Noddings, 2015, p.92). Consequently, for a female educator to diminish signs of emotional connection and caring, to assert her intellectual capacity was, initially, for Harley, a feminist act.

Harley's desire to distance herself from her students, to be challenging without being mean, to perform a white male version of professionalism, was for her a demonstration of her own professionalism and expertise. It was, however, an insufficient way of being in relation to her students. This became evident in her work with a student, Nyesha, whom she supported with developing writing skills. Harley soon realized that her work with Nyesha needed to be driven by a responsive understanding of Nyesha's concept of herself as a learner. She described Nyesha telling her "I can't do this. I'm dumb. I don't know how to do this. I'm stupider than everyone in this school. Tell me how to write this paper," and knew that she needed to work from a place of care and patience in order to support and disrupt the negative self-concept that was, among other things, impeding Nyesha's academic growth. Taking this approach, Harley realized that Nyesha and all of her students were "able to *do more* and I know that [they're] able to do more." Harley was able to see more capacity in her students from this place of caring. Valuing teaching from a pedagogy of care over a performance of white male professionalism began to emerge in Harley's becoming of an inclusive educator. Harley began to reconceptualize professionalism, or at least her own inclusive teacher professionalism, as caring. Here again, Harley had to disrupt a script she thought she was supposed to follow in order to recognize and feel comfortable with identity and practice as educator. She was once again *troublemaking* through her emergent pedagogy of care. Her rejection of white male professionalism and embracing of her self as a feminist killjoy produced, and was produced by, her practices of teaching for inclusion, and therefore the production of inclusion itself.

As Harley dipped her toes into the waters of being a feminist killjoy inclusive educator, a tragic event and the ripples of this trauma affirmed for her that caring for her students, loving them, was central to who she needed to be as an educator. In the spring of this year, Harley's student, Victor, took his own life. Harley and Victor had had a close but also frustrating relationship. She felt that their relationship was strong and "very much a mutual one" wherein he would come to her to talk about his problems and she didn't redirect the conversation to academics, but rather "would speak with him about what he wanted to speak about". They liked each other. During the parent/teacher conference that spring, however, Victor showed up with his mother and seemed "so flat, even to the point of being rude." Harley had seen Victor be rude to other teachers, but those teachers had also sometimes characterized Victor as annoying. Harley knew that Victor would assert his opinions if he didn't agree with a teacher's approach or thought that students were being treated unfairly. She did not characterize this as annoying behavior. She knew that Victor "understood what an ICT classroom was and felt frustrated by being in one sometimes," and imagined that his reactions might be interpreted by some teachers as resistant or "annoying." Perhaps she just knew him better or had a closer relationship with him, but in their interactions "he was never rude ... we were always very sweet to each other." When he was rude during the parent-teacher conference, Harley was taken aback. Still, in that moment with parents and her colleagues watching, she needed to be professional. So "instead of saying to him: Victor what's wrong? What's going on? Or are you OK?" she was "kind of cold." It upset her that Victor, with whom she had this close relationship, was acting this way but she had "to keep going. And so [she was] just going to kind of be pretty quick with him, pretty short, and move on from this."

This was the last conversation that Harley had with Victor. In processing his loss, she knew that "acting differently in that moment would not have changed anything," but she also needed to honor the significance of Victor in her life and of this experience. She wanted to understand "how can it affect the way that I live?" And so, in moving forward and finding ways to learn from and heal from Victor's suicide, Harley embraced the significance of care and moved even deeper into demonstrating love. She needed her students to know that "nothing matter(ed) more than (their) well-being" and that she needed to love them, show them that love, and name the emotion and connection of love. Harley began to develop a philosophy where "loving students" was "a radical thing" and an affective compulsion that "it would feel unnatural to be doing anything but that." She shared that "that's something that would never have come out of my mouth a couple of years ago … I never would have called it love." By coming to understand and embody professionalism as the radical act of loving her students, Harley embraced a teacher identity that was professional because it was loving. She centered love in her work as an inclusive educator, explicitly and intentionally took up her radical action against a patriarchal professionalism that she had previously adopted, and became a feminist killjoy inclusive educator to her core.

Along this journey, Harley did not waver in her commitment to inclusion. She never conceived of herself as anything other than an inclusive educator; she was a woman with a special education license teaching for social justice and equitable access to learning and participation for all of her students in a New York City high school. Her enactments as inclusive educator emerged from the process of figuring her identity vis-a-vis her attachments to scripts of "how to be" in relation to her colleagues and her students. Her push and pull toward and away from the happy housewife, the feminist killjoy, and the loving professional produced her enactments of teaching for inclusion, suggesting the need for more a complex accounting of how we conceptualize inclusion.

Harley: Five Years Later

This school year, I'm using a day calendar marketed as "inspirational feminist" that was given to me by my best friend, Liz. It includes a mix of what might be termed "white feminist" quotes and intersectional (e.g. Kimberlé Crenshaw) feminist quotes. One quote is by Alice Walker. It reads like a blessing and a tragedy: "The most common way people give up their power is by thinking they don't have any." Power exists, but it is forgettable, and often under threat of force. In her novels Alice Walker wrote about the hordes of persuasive people and systems that demand such forgetfulness, especially from people of color, in exchange for survival. She knew about the choices people make in order to regain their power and the consequences they may pay for their efforts. In my experience, schools can be engines of the process Walker describes— surrendering what is powerful—and they can also be instruments of recovery.

As a practicing feminist killjoy educator, my first impulse when I read my chapter was to bypass my narrative, question my memories, and to want to protect the men of the story. Why? Well, because our relationships improved and became healthier over time. Because those were the men who sat with me while I cried after Victor's body was found. Because I was far from perfect. Because I don't want to be disruptive and yet I desperately, obviously do. And because it is difficult to accept that I could be, at that time in my life and at any other, both powerful and drained of power.

Once Victor asked me why I hadn't said anything during a "co-taught" lesson. Victor did not obviously benefit from my support the way that other students did, and I was surprised he had noticed my silence, much less questioned it. But he did, and he led me to confront myself: I had been scared to take up space; I had surrendered my voice; I had thought myself into submission. My recovery didn't last forever, not even for the rest of the day, but in that moment, Victor drew me out. In that moment, in the five minutes between classes, Victor gave me the precious and terrifying gift that students often give their teachers, that they often can't yet give to themselves, and that it is our job as teachers to return to them in perpetuity: of staring silence in the face, of placing faith in ourselves when we feel no imperative to do so, because our imperative is to each other.

Silence is wild. In classrooms, silence can be agonizing, an excuse, a fatal lapse in responsibility. Silence can also be ethical. It can be healing and truthful. And silence can be none of those things. It can be sad, it can be empty. It can emerge from the everyday injustice of a text message telling about a child's death over the weekend. JP died five years after Victor. They were alike in their willingness to be themselves, and their selves in formation were entirely different. When Victor spoke, he risked being judged. When JP laughed, his wrongs were still there, ecstatically balanced by the light of his smile. A speaker at JP's funeral encouraged congregants not to be paralyzed by our grief. She wanted us to do two things at once, to grieve and to keep his joy alive. Victor's funeral ended with red envelopes, a symbol of new beginnings. JP's funeral ended with a song that, at its climax, emanated from somewhere I couldn't see.

But it is not uncommon in special education to trust what we cannot immediately see. If we are open to it, new definitions of ability are constantly unfolding if they are given the chance to breathe. If we look closely, classrooms are revealing places. We see a thousand triumphs in a student who is being evaluated by the wrong rubric. We see biases bleed through. The inadequacies of our educational system perennially threaten to overtake its progress. Teachers navigate a narrowly imagined, nationally perpetuated measurement of worth, with endless tools of assimilation at our disposal. Anti-racist, anti-ableist, feminist education does not deny teachers' capacity for bias, or for forgetfulness, or for hypocrisy, or for harm. But it equally does not deny teachers' capacity for change and for love. If we as teachers are unsure how to love well, if abuse or manipulation has ever masqueraded as love in our own lives, then we have to teach ourselves, because facsimiles of love will collapse in a classroom and be replaced by whatever lurks beneath. At our best, we learn how to love our students. If we never knew, we learn that power multiplies when it is shared.

References

Ahmed, S. (2010). *The promise of happiness*. Duke University Press.

Creasy, K. L. (2015). Defining professionalism in teacher education programs. *Journal of Education & Social Policy, 2*(2), 23–25.

Friend, M., & Cook, L. (1992). *Interactions: Collaboration skills for school professionals.* White Plains, NY: Longman Publishing Group.

Howard, L., & Potts, E. A. (2009). Using co-planning time: Strategies for a successful co-teaching marriage. *Teaching Exceptional Children, 5*(4), 2–12.

Murawski, W. W. (2009). *Collaborative teaching in secondary schools: Making the co-teaching marriage work!* Thousand Oaks, CA: Corwin Press.

Murray, J. (2006). Constructions of caring professionalism: A case study of teacher educators. *Gender and Education, 18*(4), 381–397.

Noddings, N. (2015). *The challenge to care in schools* (2nd ed.). New York, NY: Teachers College Press.

Pugach, M. C., & Winn, J. A. (2011). Research on co-teaching and teaming. *Journal of Special Education Leadership, 24*(1), 36–46.

Sileo, J. M. (2011). Co-teaching: Getting to know your partner. *Teaching Exceptional Children, 43*(5), 32–38.

Chapter 5

A Dystopian Tale

With Jessica Ewing

"And there's like a lot of moveable parts that never seem to sync up, that never seem to align. It seems like there's always conflict or there's always something. And [it's] always something major. And there's a complete lack of unity. So maybe like dystopian. I don't know."

Unlike the other teachers who participated in this study, Jessica's experiences seemed to have evoked ambivalence and unease rather than positive attachments. While none of the teachers whom we describe in this book claimed to have stumbled upon flawless teaching environments, their accounts were nonetheless characterized by an energy that generally signaled a momentum largely unchanged since completion of their preparatory program. They might contemplate other school environments, but their attachment to this profession was as yet, unwavering. Jessica had initially seemed hopeful about her school, but over the months, we witnessed a steady decline in her enthusiasm, and she was less able to contribute readily to the discussions in the group meetings. Jessica's story, then is not a feel-good, heroic story. Its grounding in precarity rather than certainty (Naraian, 2019), however, can offer us new ways to imagine how to begin preparing for inclusion. Her narrative, we believe, is particularly important in the questions it provokes regarding the assumptions teachers and teacher educators make about how we assess the capacity of inclusive educators. It discloses the "ableminded-ness" (Kafer, 2013) in our conceptions of such educators that privileges individual capacity rather than collective agency.

Striving for Change

It was clear from the start that the school in which Jessica began her first year of teaching was not living up to her expectations. Neither the administration, which had initially aroused hope, nor her colleagues appeared to share her disposition towards students. The apparent callousness of the former was matched by the inclination of the latter to always "blame" students. Jessica was affronted by this lack of care for students and took it upon herself to try to "change mindsets" in her school. Her goal, as she reiterated during one of the meetings, was that she wanted her students to know that "someone cares about them, that someone values them as people".

Jessica was determined to show her colleagues that students were far more competent than their teachers recognized them to be. Her confidence in accomplishing this shift was grounded in the relationships she was able to develop with the students. She recognized that she was able to elicit affirmative responses from students who, in turn, appreciated her recognition of their capability. For instance, she noticed that if she stepped out of the room, students, too, would leave and at least one of her co-teachers was seemingly powerless to demand they return. Students seemed unwilling to comply with school norms if Jessica was not present. She reported that when she left the room, the classroom descended into chaos and students were telling her "Miss, she [her co-teacher] can't teach without you there." Indeed, it was only when Jessica resumed her physical location next to the teacher that the students would quiet down.

She tried to utilize the benefits accrued by such affirming relations to support her students. Recognizing that they were adept in manipulating the situation, she approached them directly in her characteristically forthright manner. She noted:

And so I finally told some of the leaders of the classroom. I was like: 'You know you can do this faster. You know what you're doing. I see it. Stop. See how fast you can do this because she thinks you're stupid and you know it.'

And so they finally just did it. And so all these students, even the IEP ones, got it done in half the time. I said: "They are done." And she [the co-teacher] just kind of looked at me, shocked.

Despite the gratification she experienced in students' responsiveness to her, Jessica was acutely aware that these students did not produce higher quality work for her. She observed teachers who were "very, very strict" or "downright mean" to students and was unable to understand how those teachers could still evoke their students' "love." Referring to one such teacher, she wondered at the "well-managed" state of her classroom and the fact that students in her classroom were able to pass the CSA[1] examinations, a feat that she, Jessica, felt certain she would not be able to accomplish with her own students.

As the year progressed, her conviction that the school was poorly organized, the teachers mostly indifferent to the needs of students, and the administration negligent in its legal responsibilities to students began to solidify. By spring of the same year, she had reached her limit: "it's just not even like a good environment anymore. And I just want to get out." Her experiences at the school during this year had left her trying in vain to make sense of contradictions where "what shouldn't work is working; and then what should work doesn't work." She decided that she needed to renounce her first-year experience, "leave everything in the past" and move ahead. She was uncertain about continuing in this profession, but eventually she decided to remain, expressing cautious optimism during our last meeting about the new teaching position that she had found for the next academic year.

Jessica's struggles during this year emerged from the confluence of multiple phenomena. This included the distress she experienced in encountering a deficit-oriented school environment, her zealous efforts in advocating for her students with colleagues even as she came to doubt its potency for bringing about lasting change, and the concomitant anxiety about her own capability to be an effective educator. It was clear she would have benefited from more concerted experiences in curriculum planning. Strategies for reconciling competing pedagogical paradigms were also missing in her teacher preparation. Furthermore, she might have benefited from opportunities to develop her own skills as an adult educator working with and across competing belief systems.

These recommendations also assume that Jessica was solely responsible for her "success" or "failure" as a teacher. Her reflection that her experience during this year "made me really look inside myself and say 'I really don't think that this is for me'" troubled us. We were guiltily aware that as teacher educators, we too, have often secretly wondered whether the teaching profession is suitable for everyone. It would have been easy to interpret Jessica's stories as reflecting an inability to manage the routine stressors of teaching in urban contexts and as lack of readiness to enter the teaching profession. However, such an interpretation would neglect the fact that Jessica was embedded within a particular constellation of people and practices that affected her capability to enact her commitments. How did the materiality of teaching in this particular setting produce Jessica's attempts at inclusive practice? It was certainly evident that engaging school personnel with the discourses associated with inclusion was far more complex than she had anticipated. It was no coincidence that by the end of the year she noted that while it was theoretically possible to be a "radical teacher" it also meant that "I would have to completely just change who I was in order to be successful." We also wondered about her strong conviction that the people around her (particularly, teachers and administrators) were unable to fulfill their roles as caring educators. How did Jessica locate herself within those struggles? If we focused on the collectivity of elements within which her capability to act was constituted, how would we describe her efforts towards inclusion?

A Divergent Reading for Dystopian Times: Assembling "Inclusion" in Jessica's Experience

"My mentor didn't lesson plan with me, my supervisor didn't give me any feedback on the lesson plans other than "this was vague" and the administrators didn't ensure that any coursework was relevant to my needs."

The above quote was taken from one of Jessica's final dialogue journals during the late months of her preparation program. Jessica's sense of having been failed by key figures during her recently completed student teaching moved over into her challenging experiences during this first year of teaching. Her sense of self seemed to flow across multiple events, places, people and times. To better understand this movement as we saw it further unfolding during her first year of teaching, we began to read Jessica's efforts as a teacher differently. We wanted our reading to reflect the fractured nature of her own experience. We now began to attend to the many different elements within her experience that affected her capability to enact her commitments to inclusivity, giving each of them equal significance. As these elements *intra-acted* (Barad, 2007) with each other, we wondered how they constrained/enabled Jessica's efforts as a teacher? Just as importantly, how were these elements formed within such intra-action? In other words, we are suggesting that Jessica's potential to act was always in flux and contingent on how multiple elements within her experience took form in relation to each other.

To do such divergent reading, we take up the same *"diffractive" approach* that we used with Peter, to understand Jessica's subjectivity as spread over a range of different elements (Barad, 2007; Braidiotti, 2019). As we came to understand in the case of Peter, material and discursive elements are always entangled with each other. In other words, Jessica, as teacher, does not come into being separately from the students, curriculum, physical environment or discourses of learning in the school. Her "becoming" is entangled with the "becomings" of other material and non-material agents in the *intra-activity* that constituted the phenomenon of "inclusion" in her building. Our intent then, is to disclose one among many possible assemblages of entities of which Jessica is a part, that may be understood as producing the phenomenon of inclusion.

We illustrate the ways in which each of the elements within this assemblage affect, and are affected by, each other. We document the movements between them that collectively bring into being the phenomenon of inclusion. In that regard, we are less likely to dwell on what Jessica intended to accomplish, or what she was able/unable to accomplish. Rather, we examine the ways in which multiple elements intra-acted with her (and how she intra-acted with them) to understand how and what came to matter. We map Jessica's intra-activity with student-teacher relations, curricular practice, co-teaching, as well as administrative practices that eventually produced (or *mis*-produced) the phenomenon of inclusion in her building. As researchers who have identified an assemblage of entities within which Jessica enacted her commitments, we too, as we will show later, are implicated within this assemblage. In affecting and being affected by each of the various entities within this assemblage, we show how Jessica's agency to be inclusively oriented did not reside solely within her.

Jessica's attachment to her students produced them in particular ways even as it simultaneously disclosed her own assets and vulnerabilities. From the beginning, these students were "my kids" to her, demarcating them from other school personnel who treated them unfairly, whether it was in the impersonal ways in which their IEPs were developed or in the callous distribution of students across classes by the administration. Her account of her relations with students was inevitably characterized by inadequacy (hers and theirs) and the failure to meet expectations. For instance, Jessica was assigned to teach an algebra CSA exam preparatory class to students who had a history of failing the exam. She suspected that this subject had been a source of failure for herself when *she* had been a student. Even as she experienced the irony of this match in palpable ways, she also recognized that the uncaring stance of a disorganized administration to support these students perpetuated the cycle of failure. The administration's failure to be responsive to students affected the behavior of students who came to enact their student-*ness* in predictable ways, mostly through willful disengagement. She, however, continued to seek out the students who had been rejected as "the low ones." This affirmed for her the reasons why she had entered the teaching profession in the first place.

Jessica clearly experienced some degree of empowerment in her ability to elicit, at least some of the time, desired responses from students. It would not be an exaggeration to say that it was her attachment to the students that drove her efforts as a teacher during this first year. Still, the gratification she experienced in such affirming student relations remained disconnected from the rest of her experiences in this setting. It could not minimize her anxiety about her efficacy as an educator. Ultimately, Jessica's relationships with these students failed to produce the impact that she desired—they did not work diligently for her, nor did they heed her words. Her gratification in being liked by her students was not accompanied by objective academic or behavioral measurements of its impact. Most of her students continued to be unsuccessful in their academic progress and she was certain that they would fail the CSA examinations. Jessica reminisced ruefully about her successes in her previous work at a non-profit agency. In *that* setting, "I could get them [the students] to do more work or behave differently in a classroom." The connection to her current students, however, was fragile. "There started to be one [connection], I feel, in the beginning of the year, but as the year went on, I feel it kind of wasn't there." Her connection to these students was tenuous at best and hopeless at worst, given that it did not appear to happen naturally.

Jessica's entanglement with the teachers in this building was complicated. After all, they shared her working conditions of an environment that was marked by a deficit narrative of students and an absence of a cohesive culture of support for all of its members. The ways *they* were affected by this environment induced in Jessica an urgency to "change mindsets." *Her* orientation to these teachers marked them as unable to presume the competence of their students (Kliewer & Biklen, 2007). Interestingly, in a dialogue journal she wrote during her preparatory year at the university, she described similar tensions with her mentor teacher at that time, whose practices she had found troubling. Jessica's encounters within her current school carried forward some of those past misgivings about teachers' deficit-oriented responses to students. Her co-teachers, clearly, had received minimal, if any, direction in taking up alternate practices. It was no wonder that co-teaching with them was "a little hard and stressful sometimes." Still, in at least one instance, Jessica capitalized on the fact that she and one of her co-teachers were first-year educators, and initiated conversations with her on "how to speak respectfully to the students and not to be demeaning."

As a special educator, Jessica confronted the unhelpful legacy of inequitable relations between general and special education (Bessette,

2008; Naraian, 2010). The ways in which her role as special educator was taken up in this setting reflected its diminished status among general educators. Not only was she granted little time "in front of the class-room" directly instructing the students, she was most often consigned to the "periphery," working with small groups, or answering students' questions. Furthermore, to add to the indignity, she was initially denied access to student grades, because she was not the lead teacher. For most of the time, therefore, she found herself working individually with students identified as receiving special education services rather than jointly planning curriculum with her co-teaching general education partners.

Much has been written about the benefits and challenges of collaborative teaching as an important route to enacting inclusive opportunities for students in schools (Friend, Cook, Hurley-Chamberlain, & Shamberger, 2010; Hamilton-Jones & Vail, 2014). We wondered about the instruction in co-teaching models derived from that research that Jessica likely encountered in her teacher education programming. During one of the meetings for this study, participants had collectively declared emphatically that co-teaching was a much more complex enactment than they had been prepared for in their teacher preparation program. What does pre-service instruction in idealized models of co-teaching accomplish, we wondered, in the context of a setting where such ideals across all planes of experience and for all members of the community—students, teachers, administration and families—have already been compromised? Jessica 's struggles with her co-teachers indexes the need for professional development in this area for *all* teachers. However, its absence in school-wide discourse meant that this was an additional site of incapacity that Jessica could attach to herself.

The co-teaching relationships in which she found herself also did not appear to afford her the conditions for growth in the content areas with which she was unfamiliar, particularly high school math. She was particularly mistrustful of the type of pedagogical structure that was initiated by the lead teachers, such as "flipped learning" which entailed students watching a series of teacher-made videos at their own pace. This methodology seemed to be the very antithesis of her emphasis on relationships as generative for student learning. Jessica implicated the administration in this practice arguing that in actuality, it served the school's purpose to maintain order in the classrooms. She described this as a "demoralizing" form of pedagogical practice; students— particularly those with labels of disabilities—could find themselves publicly shamed via a visual tracker that listed the quizzes completed by each student. She tried to undertake "differentiation" in the midst of such asynchronous instruction, but the collective randomness or "dys-topian" nature of these practices further enhanced Jessica's own sense of uncertainty about her role. It blurred the identity she had *figured* for herself as an educator committed to social justice (Holland, Lachiotte, Skinner, & Cain, 1998).

Jessica's frustrations about her role and her uncertainties about her capabilities as a curriculum planner were also not separable from the dismissive posture of the administration in assigning its teach-ers to content area instruction. The administration backtracked on its commitment to Jessica to have her teach English Language Arts and Integrated Algebra (taught at middle schools) and instead assigned her to teach Trigonometry, Earth Science and a CSA preparatory class in Integrated Algebra. Each of these classes invoked anxiety and discom-fort in her, either because of her lack of familiarity with the content, or her presumed inadequacy to bear the cognitive load it required to understand and teach it. This in turn affected her relations with stu-dents and her co-teachers, while also evoking a harsh self-assessment of her own efficacy as a teacher. Her awareness of her own complicity in setting students up for failure—"Wow. I really set back this student because I told them something completely incorrect"—reinforced her own incapability as a teacher.

Reflecting on her experiences, Jessica recalled that much of her learning during her teacher preparation program had little applicable value. She was reminded of her less-than-successful field work during her preparatory year where she felt like "she failed every lesson plan." As she declares in the quote excerpted in the beginning of this section, this was because she received inadequate help and support throughout this process. Jessica's journal entries during her preparation are pre-scient; in one entry she wrote: "I guess I'm just concerned that that my stance will end up hurting me more than helping me when it comes to collaboration." Even as her current discomfort in engaging with contradictory belief systems was anticipated in those early journal writings, the cumulative effect of teaching in this context seemed to generate regret, even shame; the question of "what did you learn" became sadly translated into "what I *should* have done." She acknowledged regretfully towards the end of the year that she had not initiated greater co-planning with her co-teacher, even as she simultaneously expressed some uncertainty about how her efforts might have been received by that individual.

Agency for Inclusion as Precarious Rather Than Heroic

"I would rather have road bumps than teach in a way that contradicts what I believe"

Our understanding of Jessica's experiences and her agency in enacting inclusive practices, is premised on how we as DSE scholars conceptualized "inclusion" itself. Our understanding of inclusion required the discourse of an "agent of change" who must actively resist deficit-based practices. As such an agent of change, Jessica's statement above (excerpted from her journal entries during her preparatory year) admirably situates her as capable of enacting the commitments to inclusivity fostered by the program. Our own appropriation of this trope meant that initially, we directed the inquiry towards examining the extent to which she was able or unable, to accomplish the goals associated with that charge. Our approach drew on common-place understandings of inclusion in schools where a co-taught classroom is marked as an "inclusion" classroom and therefore, a critical site for the successful performance of inclusive teaching. It was predicated on understanding pedagogical practices for inclusion as informed by asset-based thinking, on relationships with students as an opportunity to disclose capacity/competence, on examinations as problematic instruments of state control, and on curriculum as a site for identity-making (Slee, 2011; Valle & Connor, 2019).

Even as these principles of inclusive teaching are important guidelines that inform the work we do, they do not tell us how the encounter with school systems affects the ways we take them up. In other words, rather than understand them as static, decontextualized principles, what if we considered them as dynamic and shifting? How would they change, with whom and under what circumstances? Within the material-discursive context where Jessica was called on to display her teacher-ness, the *apparatus of knowing* (Taguchi & Palmer, 2013) that we brought to our inquiry failed to help us understand Jessica as *more-than-human* (Bradiotti, 2019). If we simply described her efforts against pre-given principles of effective inclusive teaching, we would be unmindful of the inevitable entanglements of people and things that characterize the lived experiences of teachers. We needed to go beyond Jessica herself, and locate her as embedded in, produced by and within, a collectivity of people, ideas and practices. This would help us derive a more complex understanding of her capability to enact her commitments as well as the requirements for inclusive teaching. Our goal was not to generate a fully finished description of Jessica as a first year teacher. Rather, we have sought to surface facets of her experience that can bear significance for our collective efforts to understand inclusive teaching.

Reading Jessica's story in multiple ways helps us to begin to understand how orientations to "agent of change" can produce varied types of inclusive educators. For instance, if the discourse of inclusion was predicated on *debility* (Puar, 2017) rather than the *capability* of teachers and schools to enact inclusion, how would we describe her agency and more importantly, how would Jessica describe herself? Her enactments of teacher-*ness* might have reframed the ways we conceptualize inclusive teaching. For instance, Jessica 's summative description (below) of first her year of teaching directs us towards an alternate place to start when understanding her experiences. Her statements are predicated on the fragility of her context that was always already on the brink of failure.

> I feel like everything that could go wrong did go wrong. That's a really good way to put it, (laughs), now that I think about it .... Content wise ... it went wrong. The teachers I was paired with ... it was like two extremes. The math teacher was super organized ... but because she was super organized, it led to problems with us because *I* wasn't organized.

The conditions that can constrain/impair an individual teacher's capacity to enact beliefs and commitments do not simply constitute the external context within which those enactments occur, as though they each were separately formed (McDermott, 1993). Jessica *produced* those conditions just as she was already produced by them and within them. This is the *intra-activity* between people, practices, and things that constitute any phenomena. Her entanglement with ideas encountered at the school (and prior to her arrival at the school), with students (past and current), and with material practices in the school meant that any principles of inclusion she took up would also become part of this web and be affected by it.

Disability studies scholar Siebers (2008) suggests the we begin our analyses of human behavior from a location that privileges fragility rather than capability. Following Puar (2017), we might recognize debility as endemic to the ways in which all students and teachers experience schooling. Conditions of debility are evoked by numerous factors including among others poverty, racial injustice, inaccessible spaces, public discourses of xenophobia, hostility to marginalized populations, as well as rigid accountability mandates and procedures. We may describe the phenomenon that emerged from Jessica 's experiences, as the process of *debilitated agency* that characterizes teaching/learning in schools under current neoliberal conditions, and which impacts commitments to inclusion (Naraian, 2019). This, in turn, might deflect attention from the *competencies* that individual teachers must possess as inclusive educators to interrogating the relationships between various material-discursive entities that come to matter in their enactments of inclusion.

Jessica: Five Years Later

There were many aspects that worked against my ability to teach as I wanted to. There were five million things pulling at me all at once. I required support and unfortunately, it was not always given, particularly, in the area of behavior management; this is something that many schools apply without consistency. Grading would pile up and never end. Lesson plans that are required for everything that you do in the classroom would pile up as high as the grading pile. I found myself in relationships with parents who would use my personal number sometimes on a daily basis. Still, all these things aside, my suggestion to pre-service teachers is 'find your kryptonite and build a tolerance to it. Find that one thing that you do not have and work like hell to not let it define you.'

The story of school failure has been central or at least strongly emphasized in these preceding pages. One failure that I took upon myself is not using avenues available to me to improve my lesson planning. It was an area in which I knew I needed support. It is true that there were some avenues in my school to help me improve in this area. The Assistant Principal made herself available to us if we needed. There were many experienced teachers in the school with whom I could have co-planned lessons. However, I was unable to use these avenues and inexplicably resigned myself to play the role in which I least excelled, that is, babysitter (behavior manager) and therapist. But what I truly needed was to expand my lesson planning abilities and that is where I was unable to utilize any available supports.

If I were to do it all over again, I would tell myself: 'Push yourself to do not what is fun or what is most rewarding, but push yourself where you need it the most: your areas of need.' It is easy as a first year teacher to cling to your strengths as a much needed bubble in a crazy, thrashing sea. It is easy to say 'This is all overwhelming, let me just play to my strengths.' But it is more rewarding as an educator to watch yourself grow in an area of need than to only watch yourself build upon something that you already have some natural capabilities.

Note

1 A pseudonym for state-sponsored high school examinations whose successful completion delivered a school-leaving diploma or certificate.

References

Barad, K. (2007). *Meeting the universe halfway: Quantum physics and the entanglement of matter and meaning*. Durham, NC: Duke University Press.

Bessette, H. J. (2008). Using students' drawings to elicit general and special educators' perceptions of co-teaching. *Teaching and Teacher Education, 24*, 1376–1396.

Braidiotti, R. (2019). *Posthuman knowledge.* Medford, MA: Polity Press.

Friend, M., Cook, L., Hurley-Chamberlain, D., & Shamberger, C. (2010). Co-teaching: An illustration of the complexity of collaboration in special education. *Journal of Educational and Psychological Consultation, 20*(1), 9–27.

Hamilton-Jones, B. M., & Vail, C. O. (2014). Preparing special educators for collaboration in the classroom: Pre-service teachers' beliefs and perspectives. *International Journal of Special Education, 29*(1), 76–86.

Holland, D., Lachicotte, W., Skinner, D., & Cain, C. (1998). *Agency and identity in cultural worlds.* Cambridge, MA: Harvard University Press.

Kafer, A. (2013). *Feminist, queer, crip.* Bloomington, IN: Indiana University Press.

Kliewer, C., & Biklen, D. (2007). Enacting literacy: Local understanding, significant disability, and a new frame for educational opportunity. *Teachers College Record, 109*(12), 2579–2600.

McDermott, R. (1993). The acquisition of a child by a learning disability. In J. Lave & S. Chaiklin (Eds.), *Understanding practice* (pp. 269–305). Cambridge: Cambridge University Press.

Naraian, S. (2010). General, special and … inclusive: Refiguring professional identities in a collaboratively taught classroom. *Teaching and Teacher Education, 26*(8), 1677–1686.

Naraian, S. (2019). Precarious, debilitated, ordinary: Rethinking (in)capacity for inclusion. *Curriculum Inquiry, 49*(4), 464–484.

Puar, J. K. (2017). *The right to maim: Debility, capacity, disability.* Durham, NC: Duke University Press.

Siebers, T. (2008). *Disability theory.* Ann Arbor, MI: University of Michigan Press.

Slee, R. (2011). *The irregular school: Exclusion, schooling and inclusive education.* New York: Routledge.

Taguchi, H. L., & Palmer, A. (2013). A more "livable" school? A diffractive analysis of the performative enactments of girls' ill-/well-being with(in) school environments. *Gender and Education, 25*(6), 671–687.

Valle, J., & Connor, D. J. (2019). *Rethinking disability: A disability studies approach to inclusive practices.* New York, NY: Routledge.

Chapter 6

Searching for an Activist-Educator Self: Towards a DisCrit Classroom Ecology

With Adam Kuranishi

"I think public education is a progressive movement, but I think given the complexities of society, ableism and racism or sexism or homophobia ... [they]force us to constantly revisit what kind of progress we think we're making."

Adam was undeniably an activist. Yes, he was studying to be an inclusive educator, but he was pursuing this path as an activist; an activist committed to making societal change for people and communities that had been marginalized and oppressed. Informed by critical, anti-racist, anti-oppressive theoretical frames, Adam, a young male teacher of color, drew deeply on his own experiences to critique the ways that race and socioeconomics worked to inequitably structure society. He saw schools as a path to effect change in such inequity. Adam enrolled in his master's program in secondary inclusive education with a belief that, through classroom teaching and learning, teachers could provide marginalized youth with access to tools of power; tools that they could use to change the world around them. He had been given these tools through his education by his mentors and he wanted to continue to build that movement.

Adam was never shy to share his thoughts or conflicting perspectives with his classmates. He saw his role in this group, and perhaps in the world, to push the thinking of others, and he took that role seriously. In class, and then in group meetings during the year of this study, whenever Adam felt that a classmate might have enacted a practice that he thought was problematic or exclusionary, he would ask probing questions and provide examples from his own practice of how to do otherwise. He offered these with a simultaneous recognition that he did not have all of the answers even as he continually explored the complexities and contradictions of his practice. He believed that through this open and radically honest discourse with his colleagues, they could all grow in their understandings and practices of inclusivity.

As it turned out, activism as an inclusive educator in schools was different from what Adam had become accustomed to as a youth organizer. His prior experiences as an activist and his current role as a special educator serving as a general educator within the complex sociocultural context of his school coalesced to set the stage for a first year of teaching where the realities of racial, socioeconomic, and so-called ability disparities in education produced intractable dilemmas. To unravel these entanglements, we employ a DisCrit framework to deepen our understanding of this first year of Adam's "becoming." DisCrit, a theoretical offshoot from Critical Race Theory and Disability Studies, offers an intersectional perspective on the oppressive structures and ideologies of society that allow for a complex analysis of the way that whiteness and smartness/ability work to maintain a status quo that privileges white, able-bodied, affluent, cisgendered, males (Annama, Connor, & Ferri, 2013).

Among other tenets, DisCrit "focuses on ways that the forces of racism and ableism circulate interdependently, often in neutralized and invisible ways, to uphold notions of normalcy;" it "recognizes whiteness and ability as property" while forwarding the need for activism and resistance (Annamma, Connor, & Ferri, 2013, p.11). This nascent theoretical framework has come to serve as an analytic tool for understanding the experiences of multiply-marginalized individuals, that is, members of multiple-minority groups such as people of color *with* disabilities. Given the significance of schooling and in school experiences

for all youth, there is warranted cause for the study of the implications of this theory for teaching and teacher education. In considering
teacher education specifically, Annamma and Morrison (2018) call for
a DisCrit informed classroom ecology and offer four dimensions of
DisCrit that should be present in classrooms "designed to recognize
multiply-marginalized students" (p.73): DisCrit resistance, DisCrit curriculum, Discrit, pedagogy, and DisCrit solidarity. A DisCrit ecology
of a classroom offers a route to imagining the enactment of a DisCrit
framework in teaching. Given Adam's background, commitments, and
nuanced theoretical understanding of both critical race theory and disability studies in education, it follows that a DisCrit ecology might be
particularly generative in understanding his experience of "becoming"
as he tried to enact those commitments through his teaching practice.
What follows is a retelling of Adam's experience as a first year teacher
that specifically considers these four interrelated constructs.

Rethinking Activism from Inside the System: Resistance and DisCrit Resistance

Adam worked at Community Preparatory School (CPS), a school that
he had specifically chosen even before he was eligible to be hired. He
had chosen to work at this school because "the teachers had a lot of
space where they weren't supervised" and he interpreted that to mean
less surveillance and by extension, more independence for him to enact
greater activism in his teaching. He was also particularly drawn to this
school because the school and its community were currently navigating a complex racially charged moment in its history. The school was
co-located with five other schools on this campus. Adam described the
larger campus that had been divided into these five schools as having a
"really racist problematic reputation; at least the outside community has
looked at this school as a violent school, one that has a lot of problems,
gangs. One in which a police presence is necessary constantly." When
a new school with highly selective admissions criteria—understood by
some as a coded practice for targeting the surrounding White upper-
middle-class residents of the neighborhood—was opened in the same

building, the principal of CPS saw this as an act of racism and segregation and decided to prioritize the integration of her school. Adam was drawn to this setting for what he saw as a clear opportunity to effect change. He shared that "We're trying to counter the racist reputation. And one way in which we're doing it is through the integration of our school." He believed that the school integration was an "effort among the administration and teachers to try to develop a school that's centered around social justice and combating racial inequality." However, he was also conscious of the white parents in the neighborhood who could not afford the $50,000 a year price tag for private school and so were "experimenting and sending their child to our middle school." For Adam, CPS's explicitly stated commitment to developing a school "centered around social justice" aligned with his own commitments to racial equity and social justice. This was the kind of work he had wanted to pursue as an activist-educator. But ... he couldn't quite shake the feeling that maybe this place was less about social justice and equity than he had hoped. "Combating racial inequality" may have been a moral commitment from the school's administration, but also, affluent White people needed an affordable schooling option for their children. And so, Adam entered into this first year of teaching hoping that he was working at a school that was truly committed to social justice, a place where he could resist the status quo and work to change racial inequity through his teaching, but wary of how "radical" this space might actually be.

DisCrit suggests that societal gains for people of color and people with disabilities have largely been made as the result of *interest convergence* (Bell, 1980) wherein the interests of people of color are only structurally pursued when they align with the interest of white people (Annamma, Connor, & Ferri, 2013). That is to say, practice or policy changes that benefit multiply-marginalized students are only likely to occur, or at least more likely to occur, when they also serve the interests of their white, able-bodied peers. What is more, "the same labels provide different opportunities to students of different races" (Annamma, Connor, & Ferri, 2013, p. 17). In the case of CPS, structural changes such as increased curricular rigor, the removal of metal detectors, and more after-school programming were positioned as socially just measures to serve the school's "diverse" population but seemed to coincide with the arrival of more white students. As Adam sought to establish himself as an activist-educator at CPS, he found himself regularly grappling with whose interests he was representing and unwittingly "being sucked into the conditioning process that is inherent in the teaching profession" rather than teaching for social justice. He found himself wondering if, perhaps, the increased rigor of the curriculum and the campaign to remove the metal detectors had more to do with the white parents who were "experimenting" and sending their children to CPS than with a pursuit of racial equity.

In an attempt to organize the community for the kind of activism that he was used to, Adam advocated with his Social Studies colleagues to "invite the entire school to meet for a large assembly" in response to the shooting of Michael Brown, the Ferguson riots, and the #BlackLivesMatter movement. To him, it was clear that these current events were relevant to the student body and an opportunity for the school community to talk about race. Not everyone on the staff felt the same way, and a different group of the staff "who are more conservative white folks" advocated to "open up the gym as an alternative for students who [were] uncomfortable." Adam did not know of any students who were uncomfortable with the assembly specifically or with talking about issues of race and racism in general; none of his students had expressed discomfort to him. He was pretty sure that in actuality "other members of our staff were uncomfortable with the large assembly to talk about race." If this school was committed to social justice and racial equity, why were so many of his colleagues uncomfortable talking about race? Why were they unwilling to name their own discomfort and instead blame student discomfort for choosing to provide a sports centered alternative to this assembly? To be a transformative teacher "necessitates that teachers address their biases, [and] learn about racism and intersecting marginalizations" (Annamma & Morrison, 2018, p. 73). So, when half of the student body decided to go play basketball instead of coming together to talk about race in society and specifically at CPS, Adam was deflated. His colleagues were perpetuating the status quo, which kept his students from engaging in this racial equity work and limited his own ability to spark change. Being an activist from inside of the system could not, it seemed, look the same as it had from outside of the system.

Building from this experience and others, Adam began to question whether he had chosen the right school in which to work. He knew of high schools where they had pushed back against the standardized testing structure in this schooling district; schools, where the students were studying systems of oppression; portfolio schools—schools that opted out of the state-sponsored examinations and required students to build portfolios of their own learning instead—where students had more choice in what they studied and how they demonstrated their learning. When he spoke with colleagues at a portfolio school, he felt like he was "on the other side of the fence" from where he had positioned himself for most of his life. These colleagues would push *him* and it felt like they were critiquing him. He heard them ask, "Oh, you're teaching to the test. But, you know, why aren't you at a school like ours? Aren't you trying to stay true to your politics?" Adam knew his political commitments, he knew he was in this to fight against systemic racism, classism, and ableism, and he felt that commitment was displaced, given that he could be working in a school that pushed harder against the system than CPS. Still, he felt that CPS was working to make change and that it might be important for him to be there, in this context, pushing it towards a more radical, more inclusive reform. He began to ask himself: "do I stay at my school and try to advocate for us to be a portfolio school, advocate for more inclusive practices and an emotionally responsive pedagogy? Or do I go find a school that has those models?"

At the same time that CPS was outwardly embracing culturally responsive and inclusive pedagogies, it was also perpetuating the use and valuing of high-stakes testing that has been shown to perpetuate Whiteness and Smartness as *property* (Tomlinson, 2016). This phenomenon, in addition to the integration project of the school, seems to lend credence to Baglieri's (2016) concern that "the reforms toward multicultural and inclusive curriculum practices that have been taken up are done in ways that protect or forward White and abled privilege" because they protect "otherwise privileged children from being identified as 'at risk'"(p.175). Adam wanted to believe that CPS was a place where he could make radical change. However, as his field supervisor argued, what kept such "dungeons of oppression" alive were educators like him who misguidedly presumed that they were working toward change. In the absence of his own presence and the commitment he demonstrated to his students and his work, this school could well have been closed. In actuality, such educators, or so his field supervisor implied, were perpetuating the fatal flaws of a deeply broken system.

Committed to CPS and in the midst of the school year, Adam decided that for now, his best form of activism was to advocate for CPS to become a portfolio school that was not driven by standardized testing. His greatest ally in this project was a class parent, a "white woman who has an incredible amount of privilege who wants (CPS) to be a portfolio school." Adam was "trying to be aware" of this relationship and its dangers and affordances. He sensed her surveillance of him and his practices, as well as her entitlement but he also recognized her "influence." This interest convergence (Bell, 1980), perhaps, could be used to make the radical change he could not achieve on his own.

As Adam struggled to enact what he had formerly understood as *resistance* from this new role inside the system, he seemed to pay less attention to routine acts of resistance in which he engaged on a regular basis. Within a DisCrit ecology of the classroom the overt act of rejecting "the common deficit-oriented tropes about Students of Color that sediment bias in dysfunctional education ecologies" is resistance (Annamma & Morrison, 2018, p.73). For Adam, this practice was so innately accomplished that it did not necessarily feel like resistance. For example, when working with a student who had been in more than one physical altercation, Adam's goal was to keep having conversations with her, to understand her family history, her history, and the origins of her desire for "a persona" that "doesn't take shit from people." He believed that the most significant part of his work as a classroom teacher was "to create an environment in which people can get along and try to love each other or work with each other at least." When students cut other classes but came to Adam's history class instead, rather than reprimanding them, he let them stay and encouraged them to participate. He honored their "strategies of resistance," recognizing the "ways Students of Color traverse dysfunctional education ecologies with savvy and ingenuity" (Annamma & Morrison, 2018, p.73). Loving his students was an act of resistance. Listening to his students was an act of resistance. Valuing the gifts that his students brought to the classroom through the very nature of themselves was resistance. But this resistance did not necessarily feel adequate for Adam. His capacity orientation certainly translated as resistance through disruption of deficit driven discourses around multiply-marginalized students (Annamma & Morrison, 2018). Still, he worried whether "progressive schools" like CPS, much like the larger project of liberalism, relied too much on incremental change that was insufficient given the depth of structural racism in schooling practices (Ladson-Billings, 1998).

Constraints and Missed Opportunities: DisCrit Curriculum and DisCrit Pedagogy

A primary example of the deeply embedded structural racism and ableism of schooling can be found in the mandated curricular content and pedagogical approaches that Adam encountered at CPS. As a global history teacher, Adam was responsible for preparing his students to take a high-stakes global history exam. Even if the phrase "global history" may suggest a broad and multicultural history of the world, the content of the state-sponsored examinations was Eurocentric and unrelatable to the students whom he taught. From a DisCrit perspective, this unproblematized curricular content reified the structures of white supremacy, confirmed a false and problematic narrative that communities of color have contributed little throughout history, and perpetuated the notion that history is somehow a frozen moment in the past rather than a foundation and ongoing story of today's injustices (Annamma & Morrison, 2018).

One of Adam's primary frustrations as he began his teaching career was such curricular content. He shared that he felt "limited in terms of the scope. Like I have to focus on the world religions or Mesopotamia. I can't talk about Chicago and Brooklyn or what's happening in gentrification." He wanted to teach a curriculum that allowed him and his students to directly engage in conversations about their lives, the injustices they faced, and the ways to organize for change to fight against those injustices; he had a desire for a *DisCrit* curriculum (Annamma & Morrison, 2018). For example, when a student shared that "our school is like a prison," Adam was simultaneously inspired and frustrated, feeling that "Yeah. Schools are absolutely like prisons. And too bad we can't talk about it." He used this inspired frustration to scrap the global history curriculum and teach a unit on the school-to-prison pipeline instead. He set about designing the unit and inviting authors of a recently published book on the subject to come and speak with his students. When he brought this work to his principal, she agreed that "this (was) really important work" but wondered "how does it connect to global history" and suggested that "this would be better off done during a volunteer session during lunch." Adam described this experience as "painful" noting how important it was for his students who he worried were actually *"in* the school-to-prison pipeline" to understand what that meant and how to fight against it.

Once again, Adam wanted to enact sweeping change (Ladson-Billings, 1998) but found himself limited by his participation in the system. He had hoped that by teaching in a general education role rather than a special education role, he would have more power and flexibility to change the curriculum. What he found was that while the structures of schooling may disempower special educators in many ways (a sentiment he heard from other cohort members regularly) it also disempowered general educators when it came to curricular agency. Short of deciding to "really push portfolio" at his own school, he saw no other option than to "leave and go to another school that is a portfolio school" in order to teach curriculum that was responsive and relevant to and for his students.

Adam's experience highlights a significant difficulty of a DisCrit curriculum in that while a teacher may have the necessary commitments and desire to enact a DisCrit curriculum, depending on the context, curricular change may not always be a possibility. Annamma and Morrison (2018) suggest that "with DisCrit Curriculum, full identities and histories of multiply-marginalized People of Color are brought into conversation with dominant narratives in an interrogation of power with the goal of moving forward towards a more just society" (p.75). As a first year teacher, Adam felt that he only had the choice to enact the curriculum as it was given to him or to go to a school that would allow him to create a different curriculum. He might have missed the opportunity to teach the global history content from a DisCrit perspective, to enrich it with counter narratives and discussions of power, to "link past and present systemic injustice, instead of presenting the past as a frozen moment in time" (Annamma & Morrison, 2018, p.74). Perhaps it did not feel like a significant enough change. Or, maybe that did not feel like a sanctioned or feasible option to Adam. Perhaps, his teacher education program had not prepared him to feel competent enough to do that. Nonetheless, it filled him with anguish that "every day, I am preparing these students for this exam" instead of "resist(ing) the current model."

Beyond the curricular content, a DisCrit ecology also prioritizes DisCrit pedagogy. DisCrit pedagogy calls for teachers to design "expansive learning opportunities and multiple forms and points of assessment such that they, as teachers, can critically reflect upon and improve their practice with attention to justice" while also "shift(ing) power in the classroom" and "expand(ing) ways to hear and teach the histories of multiply-marginalized communities" (Annamma & Morrison, 2018, p.75). Beyond addressing the relevancy of the curricular content, this means employing diverse ways of sharing information and co-generating knowledge, as well as allowing for students to demonstrate their learning through multiple modalities.

The state-standards driven context of his school and the prescribed curricular content proved to present a barrier to Adam in this pedagogical practice. He knew that he wanted his class to be engaging to his students, but it was difficult to make it engaging when the content felt so removed from their daily lives. What is more, perhaps because Adam was teaching as a general educator in a general education classroom, he did not feel sanctioned to employ some of the practices to teach inclusively that he had studied in his teacher preparation program (e.g. Universal Design for Learning), practices he felt had unfortunately been understood as reserved for special education classrooms. Given these constraints, he attempted to use reflective journaling (his students teased him: "you're like the white woman from that movie-*Freedom Writers*") and rich classroom discussions to privilege student voice. It was difficult, however, to have rich discussions about content that did not feel important to his students. It was difficult for them to write substantive reflections on matters to which they were not making substantive connections.

In part, this pedagogical approach was derived from his nuanced DisCrit-informed perspective of his students and what we have described above as his DisCrit resistance. Working as a general education teacher, Adam still taught students with IEPs who had "been labeled with learning disabilities and reading disabilities and ADHD," but he understood them as people navigating the oppressive systems of schooling. For example, he described one student with an IEP and a disability label as "just a student that likes to test teachers' buttons," and often noted that maybe students had been mislabeled with learning disabilities when "other factors could be involved" such as race. And so, Adam saw the substantive work with his students as located in the relationships he built with them and the direct conversations that they had about issues in their lives and issues in the world. He shared that "what excites me is having those conversations" and then, "having the opportunity for curriculum" derived from these complex and real conversations.

In navigating the constraints of the system and seeking ways to enact his ideological commitments, Adam prioritized his relational work with students and overhauling the curricular content prescribed by the system. However, he never really seemed to find the space to reflect on how he might employ instructional approaches that privilege diverse ways of knowing and expressing knowledge. He couldn't break free from test prep instruction and build up a practice of teaching "based on student and teacher inquiry" that he felt would better serve his students. Adam shared the concern that as someone who was

> trying to address ableism as a teacher ... how am I addressing issues? Or how am I perpetuating these systems of oppression? 'Cause I have a race consciousness, right? I think about that all the time, but I don't think about ableism ...
>
> Now the text that I use, from my understanding, is accessible to every student, including the students who may read at a lower level. And there's like scaffolds that are there that every student has the opportunity to use, like

graphic organizers and such. But the labeling still exists. You know what I'm saying? So I don't know.

Adam's consciousness about his "silence or lack of consciousness" regarding disability was a self-critique of his work as an activist, his enactments of his ideological and philosophical commitments, and a worry about his instructional approaches. He knew the curricular content constrained him but he also he worried whether his own pedagogical practice was deficient.

DisCrit Solidarity

The final necessary piece of a DisCrit classroom ecology is DisCrit solidarity. Fundamentally, DisCrit solidarity is grounded in the notion that "no matter how radical a curriculum or pedagogy is, without authentic relationships in the classroom none of it matters" (Annamma & Morrison, 2018, p. 76). This meant that the teacher was responsible for building a classroom culture where students could trust each other and trust their teacher. It meant moving away from "managing" and "disciplining" students and toward understanding and supporting students. Adam deeply believed in facilitating a classroom that was "a space where students' emotional needs and development [were] being addressed." For him, this was THE paramount priority for his students, even above content knowledge. He recognized that as they negotiated the realities of their worlds, they were constantly engaged with systems of oppression in very real ways, and that their emotions deserved time, space, conversation, and exploration.

Adam enacted his commitment to prioritize his students over content knowledge through hearing their stories. He had always hoped that he could be a teacher who "could create a space where even though the curriculum might not be something that they're totally crazy about, maybe at least being in the space is positive enough for them to write their journal entry, you know?" This work was perhaps the most powerful part of teaching for him. He shared that "I cry because I'm happy, my students and I have a wonderful relationship. Or I cry because my students are dealing with a lot of shit." Building genuine relationships with his students was emotionally overwhelming for him. But it allowed him to "privilege the co-construction of knowledge, human agency and voice, diverse perspectives, moments of vulnerability, and acts of listening,"(Kinloch & San Pedro, 2014, p. 23) and co-generate a counter-storied experience for his students wherein there was a place for their voices in their school. This co-generated experience included stories about mental health, violence, trauma, and survival often times in lieu of deep study of global history content.

Such counter-storied curriculum may have felt significant to him as relational work, but it still never quite felt like he was changing enough or doing *curriculum*. He still felt that he was "learning how to construct a lesson plan and a unit, right? [To teach] content that I think is problematic." And so while he engaged in this deep and significant work with his students, he also felt himself internalizing a frustration and a sadness about not doing more, not "having a conversation generally about the role of public education or where there's room on both a larger policy level or even within a classroom level" for change. He wanted to be able to link the deep relational work that he was doing with conversations about systemic oppression and activism. He knew that there would be power in that for his students and for himself. That was, in its essence, why he came to teaching in the first place. Annamma and Morrison (2018) suggest that the integration of DisCrit Curriculum, DisCrit pedagogy and DisCrit solidarity "productively links what students face in terms of systemic oppression with what they feel about that violence; allowing them space to own their emotions and concurrently use that passion to change the system" (p. 77). Theoretically and philosophically, this had always been Adam's intention as an educator, but again, the practical enactment of it felt impossible to him. As he got closer and closer to his students and still felt unable to do right by them pedagogically and via curriculum, he could feel himself becoming disillusioned. The intensity of their emotions and experiences only exacerbated how much this work mattered, how much the system needed to change, and how inadequate he felt for not being able to do more.

As if this sense of secondary trauma was not enough, Adam's relationships with his students were also beginning to cause problems for him with his colleagues. He was often "summoned" to work with "specific students to help calm them down." Adam could feel this contributing to "somewhat of a contentious relationship with some teachers" who saw him as a young and presumptuous teacher. Adam wondered whether these teachers were unmindful of his position as a male teacher of color working with students of color and his deep and intentional relational work with his students. He was frustrated that "no one (was) willing to have a conversation about why this student may have passed my class and failed another class." He felt that some of his colleagues were not seeing the good in their students; they did not understand the power of building good relationships with them, nor the importance of building a space where students could talk about themselves and their emotions.

After one particularly difficult conversation with a colleague about this, Adam began to pull away from spending time with his colleagues and isolated himself, reinvesting in spending time with more like-minded folks, including people like Taiyo from his graduate school cohort, who he knew understood his philosophical and experiential motivations. This "reset" for Adam helped him to survive that first year of frustrations, but he knew that being the activist-educator he intended to be was not going to be possible for him in just any school context. He needed to be able to talk about the political; he needed to be able to modify the curriculum to talk with his students about the political in their lives; and, he needed a community of colleagues who could understand and support him in that work. He still wanted CPS to be that context, he hoped it could become that one day, but increasingly, he was less convinced that he could be the one to make it happen there.

Adam: Five Years Later

I left my teaching job in New York City for the suburbs after my daughter was born. My partner and I had accepted an invitation from my in-laws to move into their home on the North Shore of Long Island, the "Gold Coast." I uploaded my resume to the suburban online teacher application system after enduring several months of a grueling commute into the city. Within a few weeks, I accepted an offer to teach social studies and special education at a district only 15 minutes away from my doorstep. During this time, I began coursework toward a Ph.D. at the institution where I received my teacher education. I was eager to return to this learning community with the intention of reflecting upon and strengthening my pedagogy and theoretical analysis.

During my first month in the suburbs, I was surprised to see youth of color walking the hallways. Many of these students were in my special education courses. Consistent with statewide trends and DisCRIT research, working-class students of color are overrepresented in special education. My classrooms were some of the most racially and economically diverse spaces in the school. Like my assignment in the city, I was expected to teach a state-mandated version of history centered on white, Eurocentric, patriarchal, and middle-class norms. The small special education setting allowed flexibility in content and methodologies that allowed me to use a DisCRIT lens and inclusive strategies. The students and I studied content that de-centered whiteness by emphasizing the voices and experiences of people of color.

While the structure of schooling in the city and suburbs was similar, unique features of Long Island made teaching in my new school uncomfortable. I was startled by white suburban towns, including my school community, named after First Peoples, and disturbed that red-face caricatures of Native Americans serve as school mascots. At this time, a professor introduced me to post-colonial theory that helped me make sense of what I was experiencing in the suburbs. The "commemorations" used as town names and mascots normalize white supremacy by freezing indigenous people in the past, and position white Eurocentric narratives at the center and in the present. A colonized linear progression of history and civilization permits, without culpability, the displacement and marginalization of communities—as if the genocide of an entire people was a natural and acceptable occurrence on the land where we walk, live, and teach.

Post-colonial theorists argue that European colonial systems influence social relations, knowledge production, culture, history, and institutions beyond the existence of formal colonialism (Kerr & Andreotti, 2018, p. 56). The dispossession of the Native people of Long Island is inextricably linked to the colonial project that reproduces enduring asymmetrical patterns of power across race, class, and ability that I observe today. I integrated this epistemology into my pedagogy by engaging in a historical inquiry as part of a critical indigenous discursive analysis (Dei, 2008). While I identified the ableist and racist practices of schooling, I also sought to interrogate the ongoing processes and ideas that were engineered by colonialism. Dei, the anti-colonist scholar, proposes that framing indigenous identity "within history and outside Euro-American hegemonic constructions of the Other" works toward a "commitment to the collective good and well-being of all peoples" (Dei, 2008, p. 9). My research began with the question: "What is the history of colonialism in the region where I teach, and which narratives have been privileged and ignored?"

I learned that the sociopolitical history of indigenous and working-class communities of color on the North Shore of Long Island is long and intertwined. The dispossession of the Native Americans in coastal New York began in the mid-1600s.Within two hundred years, indigenous groups were largely eliminated by the spread of diseases introduced by Europeans, forced relocation, and wars. In the early-1800s, white settlers built large estates and named their villages after indigenous inhabitants. During this time, former slaves, runaways, immigrants, and what remained of Native tribes worked on these estates and lived in small nearby communities. Several of these communities of color were stops on the Underground Railroad and frequently encountered racial violence. Later, in the 1930s, white developers notoriously participated in red-lining practices that excluded people of color from purchasing homes. In the 1960s, Black families filed post-Brown lawsuits against North Shore school districts and federal judges forced the integration of schools. By the mid-1970s, working-class communities of color in Long Island were organizing and protesting policies that reduced the available housing stock. These North Shore communities of color advocated for federally subsidized housing, and they won.

Today, most of the Black and Latinx students who attend North Shore schools live in these historically resilient communities. Today, working-class families of color encounter continued struggles against normative conceptions of learning and ability predicated on narrow metrics of student achievement and neoliberal logic, including standardized testing. An indigenous discursive approach and DisCRIT encourage practitioners to interrogate the politics of otherness, hegemony, and oppression that are products of white Euro-American colonialism. I continue to engage in a struggle for a socially just pedagogical activist stance within our schools and among communities to interrupt legacies of power and domination.

References

Annamma, S. A., Connor, D., & Ferri, B. (2013). Dis/ability critical race studies (DisCrit): Theorizing at the intersections of race and dis/ability. *Race Ethnicity and Education, 16*(1), 1–31.

Annamma, S., & Morrison, D. (2018). DisCrit classroom ecology: Using praxis to dismantle dysfunctional education ecologies. *Teaching and Teacher Education, 73*, 70–80.

Baglieri, S. (2016). Toward unity in school reform: What DisCrit contributes to multicultural and inclusive education. In D. J. Connor, B. A. Ferri, & S. A. Annamma (Eds.), *DisCrit: Critical conversations across race, class, & dis/ability* (pp. 167–181). New York, NY: Teachers College Press.

Bell, D. A. (Ed.) (1980). *Shades of brown: New perspectives on school desegregation.* New York, NY: Teachers College Press.

Dei, G. J. S. (2008). Indigenous knowledge studies and the next generation: Pedagogical possibilities for anti-colonial education. *The Australian Journal of Indigenous Education, 37*(S1), 5–13.

Kerr, J., & Andreotti, V. (2018). Recognizing more-than-human relations in social justice research: Gesturing towards decolonial possibilities. *Issues in Teacher Education, 27*(2), 53–67.

Kinloch, V., & San Pedro, T. (2014). The space between listening and storying: Foundations for projects in humanization. In D. Paris & M. T. Winn (Eds.), *Humanizing research: Decolonizing qualitative inquiry with youth and communities* (pp. 21–42). Thousand Oaks, CA: SAGE Publications.

Ladson-Billings, G. (1998). Just what is critical race theory and what's it doing in a nice field like education? *International Journal of Qualitative Studies in Education, 11*(1), 7–24.

Tomlinson, S. (2016). Race, class, ability, and school reform. In D. J. Connor, B. A. Ferri & S. A. Annamma (Eds.), *DisCrit: Critical conversations across race, class, & dis/ability* (pp. 157–166). New York, NY: Teachers College Press.

Chapter 7

Absurdities and Contradictions: Teaching against Oneself

With Rena Matsushita

"And so showing her how it could actually be fun to teach and not have to be milita-ristic (if that's even a word), helped her kind of see what I'm trying to say. But I don't know if that's helpful. She's really just like into teaching her way and it's really hard because I'm the complete opposite of her."

Like all the other teachers whose stories we have tried to share in this book, Rena's experiences as a first-year teacher were embedded within relationships with educators and administrators who were directly implicated in the learning successes she sought for her students. We were able to identify a central phenomenon within Rena's experience that we have labeled "Teaching against oneself." To explain this, we draw on the idea of *orientations* as making bodies and objects matter. Ahmed (2010) writes: "Orientations are about how matter surfaces by being directed in one way or another" (p. 24). Being oriented towards another object not only makes it significant for some body, it also gives it form. Rena's attachment to certain ideas oriented her in a certain way to students that was generally not shared by her co-teachers. Their ori-entations towards classroom control or to accomplishing curricular objectives produced negative effects on students, on herself and even on themselves. We show how Rena identified these *mis*-attachments of her co-teachers which seemed to invoke stress rather than joy. She sought to divert those mis-attachments or introduce other attachments through *pedagogical interruptions* that could then orient teachers more positively towards students leading ultimately to a more satisfied student population.

As in our description of Peter and Jessica, we are positing inclusive teaching as a continually shifting assemblage of multiple elements that act and intra-act to deliver, in this case, Rena's enactment of an inclusive teacher, as a complex endeavor. Such an endeavor, we argue, defies simple characterizations grounded either on beliefs and commitments or in established pedagogical practices, though they certainly might include them. As we produce our version of the events and phenomena that Rena has shared with us, we locate her within these assemblages to illustrate the directions in which she moved to achieve her vision of student outcomes. Each "object" within these assemblages is continually made and remade in relation to other objects. As we have noted earlier, our goal is not to represent Rena fully or accurately through our writing (St. Pierre, 2013); rather, and not dissimilar to what we tried to accomplish with Peter and Jessica, it is to provoke new questions about inclusive teaching. *What can we learn about inclusion from thinking about Rena's practice as an assemblage? How do Rena's movements within this assemblage provoke our understandings of teaching for inclusivity?* In the following sections, we focus on three pivots within the phenomenon of "Teaching against oneself" that emerged as critical in configuring the complexity of her experience. Before we do so, we take a moment to dwell on Rena's signature response to the contradictions that she repeatedly encountered as a first-year teacher—laughter. We recognize in her laughter phenomena that we have collectively characterized as absurdities in schools.

Within the Absurdities of Practice

It was characteristic of Rena to accompany her pronouncements on school and teaching with quiet laughter that often belied the intensity of the emotional nature of the event under question. It became important for us to include her laughter as an important route to understanding the assemblage that constituted the phenomenon of inclusive teaching for Rena; indeed, it could well be part of this assemblage. We came to understand Rena's laughter not only as her means of engaging with the conditions over which she had little control, but also as a conduit for the *pedagogical interruptions* she initiated that could alter the affective dimensions of the teaching/learning context. Rena's laughter, we argue, was the effect of a desire for schooling as a happier place than it currently seemed to be. In other words, the affective responsibility of school to produce a positive environment for learning required that Rena interrupt the practices she was drawn into (Naraian & Khoja-Moolji, 2016).

Laughter generally signified the myriad contradictions and disconnects that continually found their way into Rena's everyday practice. It began with the structural dimension of her school—the school was co-located in a building which also housed the oldest high school in that borough. Yet, while *that* school remained "dark and gloomy", her own school had "bright, white walls with light blue classrooms and colorful chairs ... like everything is brand new ... giant smart boards in every classroom." The newness of her own school (a school that had been granted many liberties and release from mandatory school district policies) strangely neutralized the historic presence of the other school, making her uncomfortably aware of the structural inequality that marked the experience of the students. From the beginning, this discomfort was transferred to Rena's orientation of some suspicion towards the administration, whose practices seemed to work against its lofty vision. For instance, the school sought to provide a "college-type" experience for its students by giving them generous variety and choice in their course selection. However, the administration failed to anticipate the "scheduling nightmare" that this would produce, the resolution of which was placed on teachers who had to work long hours to rectify the errors. Indeed, when teachers like Rena advocated on behalf of their students, they were ironically rewarded by being expected to reconfigure the school schedule. The principal professed support for students in special education, but the workload placed on special educators like Rena was so intense they had little opportunity to truly support those same students.

Rena's laughter when describing all these instances signaled not only the absurdity evoked by the contradictions within each situation, but also, implicitly, an awareness of the administration as powerful, even stealthy and far from benign. Her laughter constituted her as an "affect alien" (Ahmed, 2010) where she was unable to respond in the way that she was expected to; she could not react positively to the conflicting orientations to students and teachers that the administration continually displayed through its policies and its expectations of teachers. For instance, when assigned to teach students literacy skill remediation after they had been promised arts-based courses, she was, incredibly, expected to ignore the likely anger and frustration of the students (who were expecting creative and engaging course content) and focus solely on remediating their content area skills. The gap between the vision and the reality remained too wide and the school was unable to evoke the required attachment in Rena to its role as a positive learning space. Laughter permitted Rena to acknowledge that disconnect while neutralizing its potency to disrupt her own affective orientation to her work, in particular, to the students. (In a subsequent section, we describe her affective orientation to settings as separate from her attachment to students).

The disconnects acknowledged by her laughter were just as apparent in her pedagogical responsibilities. Rena found herself engaged in a continuous struggle with teaching curricular content in subject areas that were difficult for her, particularly chemistry and biology. The incongruity of being placed in a position of supporting students with disabilities in a content area that she likely failed when she was in high school was further exacerbated by the unreliable planning styles of her co-teachers. As she noted, "when we co-plan, a majority of the time my co-teachers are planning out what they're doing and I am trying to understand chemistry (laughs)." Not receiving their plans ahead of time meant that Rena was unable to grow her own understanding of the content, let alone plan modifications for students in the class who might need supports in learning. The distance between what she was supposed to enact as a special education teacher in a high school content area class and her available knowledge in that area oriented her differently to her co-teachers. We show later how, instead of helplessness, the laughter evoked by that gap oriented her affirmatively to her colleagues as well as to her students.

Assemblages for Inclusive Practice

Rena's experiences as shared with us are particularly evocative of the collectivity of elements that marked her inclusively oriented practices. The construct of *assemblage* to understand social phenomena typically draws on the work of the philosopher Deleuze (DeLanda, 2006).[1] Rather than considering entities (whether individual persons, organizations, species, or other forms of matter) as self-contained discrete organisms, a theory of assemblage examines them as collectivities formed through and within relations with each other. Institutions such as schools are assemblages certainly of the human bodies (students, teachers, families) that inhabit them, but other entities such as the building architecture, its physical location in the neighborhood, the food served in the building, the curricular texts used in classrooms, for instance, are equally parts of the assemblage. The capacities exercised by entities (e.g. families or texts) within one assemblage (a school) may not be realized similarly in another, given that the relations between parts of *that* assemblage are differently constituted.

In the following sections, we examine the assemblage(s) of inclusive practice that emerged through Rena's stories. Rena's capacity to affect others (her students, her co-teachers, the administration) was affected by the relations that existed between each of them.

How Settings Come to Matter: The "Good" and the "Bad"

> Setting is really important. Like this year teaching in a high school, and the two years at [Sheepshead Bay] high school in Brooklyn, I don't think I cried as many times I did in the total of those three years than I did last year [Residency year] in the middle school setting. I might have cried I think like (laughter) every day until that job ended.

Rena almost decided not to become a teacher. Despite her prior experiences with gang-related youth in schools and with students in self-contained classrooms, her residency year in her teacher preparation program proved to be difficult. It presented a challenging mix of demanding teaching routines, students whose struggles presented as strange to her, and the discouraging stance of her university-based mentor. The distress she felt during her student teaching year, however, did not transfer to her students. As she insisted, "I loved the kids. I love working with all kids. I think that that's something I can definitely say." But it did evoke doubts about her competency, delineating teaching as a profession that was not suited for her. Her decision to return (almost at the last minute) to complete her credentialing requirements was prompted by a re-assessment of her own capacity, which she recognized as related to the setting.

> If you think back, it's like, it has to have been the setting 'cause I taught algebra for two years at Sheepshead and I was totally fine cause that was like my comfort level. Right? And I'm teaching chemistry now, which I failed twice in high school. It stresses me out and I definitely have to study chemistry a lot more than probably the students are studying for me right now. But I'm still totally fine with teaching it.

Rena's search for her competency directed her towards her own and others' activities in her school settings. She acknowledged that content area knowledge might be a source of some stress, but that alone was insufficient to evoke a completely negative orientation to teaching. She tried to explain her distress the previous year. "Last year, [Residency year] they hated-, they hated SPED in that building. My mentor teacher just really is a good person but wasn't a good teacher." The antagonism towards special education in the building merged with the incompetency of her mentor teacher to collectively produce a setting that was "the worst place to work." Not surprisingly, there was little in this setting that could provoke a positive orientation—"it also didn't have anything that I loved to do"—affirming for her that her competency was entangled with the setting.

Rena acknowledged the unpredictability of settings, the demands they placed on teachers as well as their capability to evoke a positive attachment towards them. Such unpredictability left teachers in a vulnerable position producing some disequilibrium. She stated emphatically: "Every time your settings change, something uncomfortable happens." The only way such precariousness could be mitigated and a positive orientation to teaching re-established would be to ensure "there has to be some kind of comfort for you" in that setting. In the absence of that, it would be impossible to continue.

She would need to uphold this dictum in her present school. Increasingly, her guarded orientation towards the principal had evolved into increasing outrage at his volatility and bouts of rage directed at her and her students. Yet, she was able to say at the end of that first year, "If you can just ignore that person, it's a really good environment." Even as the apparent "craziness" of the principal repelled her, "school" could still be constituted as an object of desire outside of leadership/administration. The *good*ness of the school setting was evoked by other configurations of people, relations and ideas that did not depend on the capability of the principal alone to evoke a positive orientation to the school. For instance, her co-teachers were "annoying," the students were "good," and the staff were still largely "good". *Their* good*ness* allowed her the confidence to say, "there's not a single teacher in our building that will ever put themselves first over a student." With "great" counselors and a dean that was "super into social justice," the cumulative impact of the assemblage was sufficient to caution her from taking the risk of going elsewhere where she could "end up with another bad principal." The school as a whole invited optimism for its students' outcomes.

Still, the *good*ness of this environment could just as easily be made vulnerable by elements in the assemblage that were continually evolving. For instance, old race-related tensions between some groups of students erupted in the school during the year of the study, leading to moments of tension for staff and students alike. Rena's decision to continue working in this environment stemmed from her adjudicating between "bad" and "good" environments. Her interest in gang-related youth and her prior experience working with them produced these events as interesting, even normal, rather than fearful. For Rena, then, the *bad*ness of an environment was prompted by the extent of "challenge" invoked by students, and/or the intensity of violence it brought about. The "challenge" presented by students in this school—"a kid brought a knife in"—invoked a lesser degree of *bad*ness. Given the otherwise generally "calm" student population, such events were "no big deal."

Still, students were required to present some level of "challenge" for the setting to be considered "good." This was clarified during her Residency year;

> And then last year in middle school, I was just like [to students]: Why are you crying? (laughter) I don't know how to solve your going-to-the-bathroom problem. I'm sorry. (laughter)

The scale of trouble in this (middle school) setting was woefully minimal in comparison to her prior work with gang-related youth. It produced students in this setting as not "challenging" enough; her aversion to their insignificant problems spread alongside the stress of her workload and the repeated assessments of her incompetence by her university-based mentor described earlier, to intensify her distaste for this setting.

For Rena, it did not matter if the school itself was non-functioning. Instead, "it's the population of students that I'm focusing on." For instance, gang-involved students were saturated with the pleasurable affects of her own memories working with them that transferred easily to her sense of capability as an educator. Settings then were never only about students or staff or about the administration. They were part of the assemblage of events, ideas and affects that they produced, and which produced them.

Pedagogical Interruptions

Rena's focus on the students as the driving force for professional goals, meant that the impetus for her activities as a teacher were always directed at orienting students to school in positive ways. Her starting point was to re-orient her own stance towards the foundational premise of teaching students with labeled disabilities—the issue of "need."

The IEP says they <u>need</u> these things ... like, they <u>need</u> a graphic organizer, or they need *this* to learn. But I kind of started teaching backwards in my literacy class ... So what I do is instead of focusing on their literacy needs, I focus on what they like to do. And that way, as they're more engaged, they're working on writing without even knowing ... And it's not that they need these things. They don't need a graphic organizer. They just need engagement or some form of interest.

Beginning with students' affective orientation to the subject permitted Rena to creatively manipulate her pedagogy to interrupt the negativity with which curricular subjects arrived saturated in this building. Such negativity might originate in prior attachments of failure to the subject, or in the coercive assignment by administration to courses not chosen voluntarily. Discounting hopes of getting students invested in school ("I think that's a battle we just can't win"), she instead focused on getting students invested in each of the classes they were in. For example, she might begin a remedial reading class by teaching students how to write their names in graffiti. Following this with a project on learning the history of their names that might include learning from family and/ or members of the community produced greater student investment in their learning. Rena found that such arts-based pedagogy—whether graffiti, painting or origami—was most likely to produce "crazy" results, where students unbelievably oriented positively towards the subject at hand.

In Rena's account, "crazy" pedagogy meant interrupting the assemblage of texts, students, failure, success, materials, learning outcomes, teacher priorities, to create a new assemblage where a range of materials and practices, academic and non-academic, could produce new phenomena of learning/engagement. She discovered that not all students were keen on taking up the traditional arts as an entry into content area learning. But "non-artsy" materials that were "more like hands-on art" could produce interest in students. Pedagogical interruptions might simply mean instating regular mini-labs before an actual chemistry lab that then provoked enough curiosity to accomplish a higher rate of completion of required work. Or, it was a turn away from algebra to a focus on mental math that could produce overwhelming success on the state high school examinations. It was the dramatic positive shift in engagement evoked by these methods that constituted the "craziness" of such instruction. Students could arrive at completely different relations with a typical biology class because content was reconfigured so that they could "learn about bacteria and DNA and RNA stuff, but we do it through Michael Jordan [and] Russell Wilson." Or, "Now we are doing sickle cell; so deaths in NCAA through sickle cell ... all sports-related. Kids love it. It's crazy." The unbelievable enthusiasm evinced by students for the "new" assembling of content transferred itself to the type of pedagogy that was able to produce results—its power to accomplish results was "crazy."

"Crazy" pedagogical interruptions turned predictable instructional priorities on their head by centering the students and producing "fun." Sometimes, that might mean turning away from the content. So, if her co-teacher did not appear to have a coherent plan for the moment and the class was in disarray, "I'll just pick on a random student who doesn't seem like they're at the most happiest time and just sit with them and talk ... talk about life." Or, if she had been abandoned by her co-teacher (which happened in biology) and a fight had erupted in the classroom, she elected to lower the intensity of the situation by putting on music, encouraging students to talk to each other, while she herself focused on talking with a small group. She reasoned that "at least that group of kids had something in that class other than just talking to their friends."

In each instance, Rena interrupted the flow of apathy from either the students or from the teacher to manipulate the affective orientation of students to school and learning. Such manipulation accomplished the transformation of *need*—whether Rena's or the students'—into greater capability. So not only were students demonstrating success in school via greater rates of completion of work, and higher levels of understanding of content, their success attached itself to her producing a greater sense of "competency" in herself as a teacher. Once they were engaged in the learning, there was little need for her to "discipline" or "beg" or continuously remind them to be doing something or the other; their investment in the learning "alleviate[d] so much stress in general." The main pivot on which Rena's instructional and curricular decisions rested was clearly the students.

Co-teaching for Change, Changing Co-teachers

> The kids hated this teacher. The kids just walked out. By the time the class
> ended, she may have had five of the 30 kids left in there. Cause they were so
> frustrated. …And she really, really thanked me afterwards for coming in and
> like helping alleviate that tension and kind of bringing in a lighter look.

A recurrent theme in Rena's stories of her co-teaching relationships was
change; changes in herself, the situation, the students, and of course,
her co-teachers. These trajectories of change began with disaffected
students and or disaffected or hopelessly ineffective teachers. She discovered that her orientations to pedagogy were markedly different
from her co-teachers and her struggle became one of persuading them
to shift their orientations such that it could interrupt the cycle of dis-
affection in the classroom. After initial disequilibrium, therefore, Rena
initiated a process of change which then produced "thankful" teachers
and "happy" students.

Rena repeatedly described the effects of teachers' orientation to
content knowledge as unsuccessful for student learning. For instance,
the chemistry teacher was extremely knowledgeable, really "intense",
but unable to recognize when students were frustrated or that they
were out of their depth, leading to a situation where they simply left the
classroom. Rena's intervention to introduce pedagogical practices such
as visual modifications to the chemistry teacher's PowerPoint slides
and worksheets evoked greater interest and understanding on the part
of students. Additionally, she deliberately "slowed her down" by notic-
ing signs of students' frustration and drawing the chemistry teacher's
attention to it. Rena's pedagogical intervention with her co-teacher was
aimed at altering the affective dynamics of the classroom.

Unlike her co-teacher, Rena's assessment of classroom learning was
driven by her orientation towards students as learners—they required
scaffolds to enter the space of learning. Her affective engagement with
the students was in marked contrast to the "strict" chemistry teacher
who relied instead on compliance to rules of behavior and by Rena's
account, rarely smiled. Initially, the encounter with a colleague who
was negatively disposed to students and who applied rigid classroom
behavioral norms, coupled with the impermeability of a subject matter

that evoked the anxiety of failure in her, caused an outraged Rena to be dismissive of this teacher. Learning to view her adult colleagues as learners eventually oriented her more generously towards the teacher, thereby lessening her own stress. After initiating conversation with her co-teacher about how she was "losing the students", Rena sought to actively co-plan with her to break up the monotony of "study, study, study, lecture, lecture." She initiated more intermediate steps in the pedagogical process that broke down the complex ideas that the teacher formerly might have delivered through "a giant packet." As students' attendance patterns rose and they began to express greater understanding of the subject, their engagement spread to infuse Rena's co-teacher with excitement; she became "really happy." By the end of the year, "the kids loved her," they were all in attendance and "it was a really successful environment." Rena played a catalytic role in the manipulation of affect in the room such that the negativity that drenched both students and teachers was transformed; not only did it move from a class she knew students hated to a "successful environment," it produced a teacher that students could love. Such a positive re-orientation was now received by the chemistry teacher as gratitude for Rena's presence. As Rena's affective re-orientation to her co-teachers produced "happy" students and "thankful" co-teachers, she also noted a surge in her own capacity. She admitted to a sense of pride in thinking about these successes in a subject that she herself had failed twice in school.

Even as the teacher's "unknowing" of inclusive pedagogical practice proved necessary for the redistribution of affect in this classroom, Rena's own "unknowing" of *subject matter* also served to cement that process. She served as the "benchmark" against which her co-teacher could assess the appropriateness of the instructional content. In other words, as Rena noted: "If I don't get it, that means kids aren't really going to get it." Her co-teacher's resulting positive re-orientation to students and to her pedagogy now produced a work context that was marked by being "easy" in that "she's all for changing anything she's made, making it better." The success of the process of change initiated by Rena affected both teachers; it allowed Rena to delineate her colleague as a "good partner" while also establishing herself as a competent teacher, despite her lack of proficiency in content knowledge.

Her relationship with her co-teacher for biology produced a different "extreme." She was not shy about expressing her reaction to him: "I really disliked working with this man. Like everything he does is against my teaching." Still, she could also confess to some ambivalence about him—his interest in building relationships with students drew her to him and his personality matched her own. Yet his unstructured pedagogical practice conveyed indifference to what students learned and made her fume. It produced large blocks of time when students idled; his unpreparedness for class, dependence on prepared materials available online that he simply "handed out" to students, and refusal to co-plan with her, outraged her further. As a final insult to students, he followed an arbitrary form of grading that bore no relation to what students had accomplished. The situation was complicated by the fact that many of the students warmed to him precisely because of the freedoms they were given; freedoms that, Rena argued, produced little learning.

For Rena, the co-teacher's practice was a mis-enactment of teacher-*ness*; without a plan, it just produced "forty-five minutes of nothing." A month into the second semester of co-teaching with this teacher, she decided to take matters into her own hands; she informed her co-teacher that she would take over the unit, "because you don't have anything anyway." Despite the *nothingness* generated by his teaching, or maybe because of it, she oriented patiently towards him: "I explained everything. I explained areas in which I can help. I told him areas in which I can't do 'cause I don't understand biology." Rena's own attachment to inclusive teacher-*ness* required that she orient towards her co-teacher as a learner.

Her co-teacher eventually responded positively to her efforts. With his cooperation, she began to make suggestions about how to break down his instructional plan and the content. Those efforts paid off not only to deepen her own attachment to his class but also in orienting her co-teacher to more student-centered pedagogy. "And he was really thankful and started to plan with me." He began to involve her more in curricular planning. However, if such planning did not happen, "it goes back to 45 minutes of nothing." For this teacher, at least, the classroom was situated on the brink of *nothingness*. "I enjoy helping him and supporting him. But I don't think he's learning." Still, Rena's attachment to enabling his teacher-ness held strongly: "I plan to go till the end." She accepted too, the prospect of co-teaching with him the following year. Her positive orientation to activating his teacher-*ness* was intensified after learning about the positive recognition *he* achieved during his teaching evaluation (he deliberately selected the class he co-taught with her as the site for this evaluation).

The many different disconnects or contradictions between what should have happened and what did actually happen, evoked laughter throughout her telling. Rena, we concluded, found herself in this classroom teaching unfamiliar content alongside a teacher who swung between indifference and commitment, a student body that desired both the "nothingness" of his teaching as well as rebelled against it, and an administration that showed little foresight in the placement of students. In this assemblage, Rena's laughter signified the maintenance of a positive orientation to school that was itself fueled by an affirmative stance toward teachers who required support from her to create positive learning environments for students. At the end of the year, Rena was assigned by the administration to serve as a coach for special educators in collaboratively taught classrooms during the following year. Even as this evoked puzzlement—"It's really hard for me to figure out what that role means for me next year"—it re-affirmed her fundamental orientation to students and teaching.

Rena: Five Years Later

Laughter is created from the environment in which people exist. If a school is well known for its violence, suspensions, and low scores then naturally, students entering that building will come with these negative preconceptions. During that first year of teaching, my school grappled with these questions: What is within our control to alleviate stress? What can be done to create an environment which induces laughter, joy and therefore daily success? The principal clearly had a vision to create a welcoming space for students and to combat existing negative preconceptions and history of this building. Through the chaos and exhaustion of that first year, I found my areas of laughter and light. The constant reminder that I was helping my students ultimately kept me going. I felt glad that my extensive knowledge of each of the special educa- tion students in the building was being utilized in order to create a successful environment for them. I knew that the teachers were overly stressed, but I also wondered what that meant for the students. I created signs on my classroom door with "office hour schedules" where students could come in during that time to convey their frustrations. More and more teachers began to enjoy this idea and offered "office hours" as well. This led to less chaos in the halls and a deeper understanding of how we as a school can continue to create success within our lofty vision.

By the end of my second year, I had learned that the principal's rage was due to the stress of trying to create the perfect school; it was not ill-hearted. I began to try and learn how to work with the principal instead of ignoring and keeping to myself: "I need to combat what's making me uncomfortable because I enjoy working here and ignoring my discomfort will not make it better." I began to observe my principal as if observing one of my students. You should never choose to ignore a student that you may be having difficulties with, so why should I do that to my fellow staff members? I learned his strengths and weaknesses and began assisting in areas he needed most. By the end of my third year, I could only see the brilliant visionary who will go to great lengths in order to create a unicorn school. I also became one of his most trusted staff members and was relied on throughout the school. The creation of trust goes a long way to feeling comfortable in a setting.

Inclusive pedagogy, for me, is the process of constantly questioning what I am doing: Am I meeting the needs of all the students in my classroom? Am I working in the most optimal way with my co-teachers? Am I teaching in a way that students want to come back to my classroom tomorrow? Am I find- ing things I love doing so that I also enjoy coming back to my own classroom? I chose to be a special education teacher because I feel like we have the power to be creative in areas that general education teachers may not have the time or the energy to do. I enjoy creating curriculum, but I most enjoy recreating existing curriculum to make a classroom student friendly. Balancing every- thing a teacher is expected to teach within the year with activities and experi- ences in the classroom is ultimately what makes me thrive. Students can learn from worksheets and books, but the knowledge gained from actual experiences, I believe, stick with them throughout their years.

After all my experience working with hundreds of students, I've learned that there will always be numerous ways in teaching one thing; figuring that out in a way that fits the students I have currently is what I chose to commit to as a teacher. I find enjoyment in the challenge to be different and to learn from my students as they are expected to learn from me. Every year there will be a different set of students and with that comes different challenges and outcomes. If they are constantly changing, then I, too, have to prepare myself to constantly change as well. I believe the same mindset goes with my co-teachers. Adults are learners just as much as students (laugh). Creating an environment where everyone is eager to learn will accomplish much more than force feeding knowledge into them. Teaching should become more and more enjoyable as one gains experience. I think all the stress and exhaustion the first few years was me trying my to figure out the educator I want to be.

Note

1 "Assemblage" has strong parallels with the notion of apparatus used by Barad (2007) to illustrate the intra-activity of multiple "agencies," which we employed to explore Peter's and Jessica's experiences.

References

Ahmed, S. (2010). *The promise of happiness*. Durham, NC: Duke University Press.

Barad, K. (2007). *Meeting the universe halfway: Quantum physics and the entanglement of matter and meaning*. Durham, NC: Duke University Press.

DeLanda, M. (2006). *New philosophy of society: Assemblage theory and social complexity*. New York, NY: Continuum.

Naraian, S., & Khoja-Moolji, S. (2016). Happy places, horrible times, and scary learners: Affective performances and sticky objects in inclusive classrooms. *International Journal of Qualitative Studies in Education, 29*(9), 1131–1147.

St. Pierre, E. A. (2013). The posts continue: Becoming. *International Journal of Qualitative Studies in Education, 26*(6), 646–657.

Reflections on Agentive Maneuverings[1]

For most novice teachers, the transition into the first year as a teacher of record generates a range of emotions (excitement, apprehension, anxiety, confidence, resentment, surprise) and the teachers in this book were not unique in the process they experienced as they navigated the surprises and challenges of their first year of teaching. What has been particularly instructive for us, as *their* former teachers, are the ways in which their stories have confirmed the unpredictability of the trajectories of practices brought on by commitments to inclusion; they have compelled us to draw on a range of theoretical frames to help us understand their *becomings* with greater complexity. For each one, the commitment to be an inclusive educator was never in doubt; yet, the continual encounter with complex, multi-layered situations in schools produced an affective orientation to that identity that left its meanings in flux and as never self-evident. In that regard, we are struck by the unmistakable stance of self-reflexivity adopted by each of them. Though we were well aware of this during their pre-service program of study, their continued reflections on their practice (of which we have a mere glimpse in their writings for this book) are a reminder that our work, as researchers, relies on their capability for such practice, without which this book may not have been possible. For that, we are deeply grateful to Taiyo, Molly, Peter, Harley, Jessica, Adam, and Rena.

Reconciling Narrative Agency with De-Centering Moves

We began this book project with a firm commitment to document the stories of our participants and to privilege their understandings of their experiences as novice teachers. We were unwilling to hold them to any pre-determined standards or notions of competence as inclusive educators. Rather, we sought to describe them in ways wherein they could recognize themselves; additionally, we hoped to offer some tools that might add other dimensions to their narratives that they may not have considered before. In that sense, we see our work in recognizing their stories as a form of intervention (Clandinin & Connelly, 2000).

As we sought greater complexity of their stories, we felt compelled to draw on multiple frames besides disability studies, including Critical Race Theory, DisCrit, affect theory, assemblages, new materialist ontology, as well as culturally responsive teaching, that could help us retain our commitments to both teachers and students while also broadening the scope of our analysis. We acknowledge that some of these frames, as we have explained in those chapters, de-center the individual agent—a phenomenon that may seem to contradict our concern for their stories. We deemed this move necessary to complicate our own understandings of what inclusion might mean. An important goal of documenting the *becomings* of our participants was to leave ourselves open to surprise in coming to know inclusion. We were simultaneously determined to preserve their voices in the development of this work. Our rendition of their experiences then straddles these seemingly oppositional epistemological stances (Ellingson, 2011); we both center and de-center our participants to disclose the complexities of inclusive practice in different contexts.

The stories of Taiyo, Molly, Peter, Harley, Jessica, Adam, and Rena have accompanied our own journeys as teacher educators and researchers since the completion of the study. Undoubtedly, this work continues to inform our practices with novice teachers as it has also disclosed new trajectories for inquiry. In this chapter, we identify some themes that have surfaced for us in the exploration of their experiences and which we hope can deepen our understanding of not only teacher preparation for inclusive education but teacher education, more broadly.

Teacher Competence for Inclusion

At the heart of the struggles of these teachers during their first year lies the claim to competence as an inclusive educator committed to socially just practices. For most of them, such claims had to be understood and recognized in the context of complicated relationships with colleagues who brought differing conceptions of their roles as inclusive special and general educators. In other words, their *figured* identities as socially just inclusive educators had to be continually negotiated alongside their *positional* identities as teachers struggling against unexpected hierarchies of gender, knowledge, and experience prevalent in schools (Holland, Lachiotte, Skinner, & Cain, 1998). While tensions produced therein could be "productive" (Stillman, 2011), they also suggested that their work during this year was particularly precarious (Naraian, 2019).

The disconnect between their figured and positional identities directed us to a more materially informed analysis of their experiences. It made it impossible for us to attend only to discourses of schooling in their stories and the ways those discourses construct normalcy and inclusion/exclusion within their settings. Instead, as we documented their affective orientations to their practice and the assemblages within which they were produced, we were inevitably drawn into the ways in which settings came to matter in their enactments. We came to know and understand teacher competence differently.

Teacher Capacity at the Interface of the Individual and Social

For each teacher in this book, understanding one's capacity was inseparable from what was made available within each school setting in which they practiced. Said differently, the bumping of their personal "stories to live by" with the "stories of school" (Clandinin & Connelly, 1996) produced the conditions within which they would have to carry out their commitments as inclusive educators. Needless to say, such conditions were unpredictable and not always in sync with the priorities they brought as educators. At the same time, each teacher was also being evaluated by administrative superiors who drew on an individualized conception of teacher capacity that privileged mainstream notions of teacher knowledge, disposition, and skills. Indeed, the widely used Danielson rubric for evaluating teacher performance in many school districts in the US is premised on a decontextualized, ahistorical set of competencies that individual teachers are expected to possess regardless of the contexts in which they teach (Danielson, 2016).

Such evaluative rubrics are framed largely from a "first-order perspective" (Sandberg, 1991; cited in Huntly, 2008), where those not currently engaged directly in the everyday work of teaching have determined the skills, disposition, and knowledge that teachers require. Besides a reliance on capacity as an individual property, such frameworks carry forward standardized notions of competence that have been critiqued as encouraging compliance and conformity rather than innovation (Stevens, 2010). In their oversimplification (if not gross negligence) of the daily local complexities which collide with elements of evaluative rubrics, standardized notions of competence leave little room for acknowledging the fluidity inherent in the practice of teaching that is born out of having to continually navigate contradictory priorities and phenomena. Additionally, as Stevens points out, the element of power which our participants clearly experienced in relation to their colleagues and/or their administration is obscured within such standards.

If, as we noted in the Introduction, teacher agency for socially just practices is an *achievement* that is accomplished through practice rather than a capacity within individuals, a standards-model of competence that has characterized both pre-service and in-service teacher assessment only minimally implicates the multiple overlapping phenomena of teaching corroborated by the teachers in this book. In privileging

a static notion of capability, it fails to account for teachers' own relations with their performance. For instance, Peter's understanding of
capability that we have identified as a form of "deferred competence"
expresses recognition not only of its continually evolving nature, but
the conditions within which that surfaces. It captures with more complexity the cumulative benefits of experience that renders competence a
forward-looking construct that can never be fully available at any given
moment in time.

Current understandings of competence are premised on notions of
inclusion solely informed by abstract notions of equity and justice that
direct us to consider such competence as residing *within* teachers—they
either have it or don't—which evokes a deficit-based approach to teacher
learning. However, an understanding of inclusion that recognizes it as a
complex material-discursive phenomenon will recognize that teachers'
agency to enact it is also deeply situated. It cannot simply be presumed
to flow readily from strong beliefs and commitments to equity. Instead,
situated agency emerges from the collectivities that constitute the immediate social context against which teachers' performances as educators
are measured (Danforth & Naraian, 2015). These collectivities include
the hierarchies determined by race, socioeconomic class, gender and
professional status between teachers and their students (and their families), between general and special educators, between novice and experienced teachers, and between schools and state-enforced standards of
competence.

Among all the teachers in this book, we saw the continual movement between practices they ruefully recognized as ableist and more
humanizing approaches that they could take up when they were able to
exercise greater autonomy. Such ideological movement may be inevitable in the negotiations that take place daily within schools. In the everyday context of schools, it testifies to the capability of teachers to remain
reflexive in the context of debilitating political priorities, to make decisions that are informed by adjudicating competing beliefs with care for
students and their families, and to simultaneously recognize the need
for self-preservation. Teacher competence as a fluid attribute remains
entangled within the personal and the social.

Teacher Identity and the Relationship between Inclusive Education and Special Education

In one sense, this book (and the study that prompted it) has been an opportunity for teachers to reflect upon and understand their own competence. If teachers' own sense of competence must be granted a legitimate place in the discourse on teacher capacity (Huntly, 2008), then it needs to be acknowledged that the contexts within which they achieve such competence encompass both general and special education. Said differently, any understanding of teacher capacity for inclusion must account for the relations between general, special and inclusive education. While as researchers, we may be able to cleanly disentangle these separate threads, it is much harder, if at all possible, to do so in practice.

Historically, schools' responses to students' learning differences, whether presumed biological or derived from social markers such as race/ethnicity, socioeconomic class, or linguistic status, have been to utilize the concept of "special educational needs" as a means to advance the rights of historically marginalized learners (Florian, 2019). This, of course, has necessitated the entanglement of special education within discourses of inclusive education. Even as this remains a source of discomfort to inclusive education scholars who are justifiably wary of the deficit-based discourses that accompany the former, it is also increasingly acknowledged that inclusive education is ultimately a process towards more egalitarian systems that will inevitably be expressed differently under varied sociocultural contexts. As Florian (2019) explains, the very ambiguity of this process itself means that how special education is practiced alongside inclusive education remains unclear and contingent. Too often, it would seem that the focus on individualized needs/pedagogy that is a hallmark of special education sets in motion practices that perpetuate forms of exclusion. While some researchers call for a radical reimagining of special education (Booth & Ainscow, 2002; Florian, 2019), the *decoupling* of these systems envisioned by others (Slee, 2011) equally remains out of reach. Inclusive education and special education are simply unhappily bound together.

Not surprisingly, inclusion remains a contested term that appears to have lost its "insurrectionary edge" (Graham & Slee, 2008). For teachers such as our participants who must encounter this coupling at every moment, the call to remain inclusive in their teaching is not easily met, even as it drives their practice. They were formally prepared to serve as inclusive educators within educational systems that are unambiguously premised on the separation and categorization of differences that are perceived as inhering within students (Slee, 2011). The relationship between these systems (general and special education) then, is crucial in the configuration of their own sense of competence. As special educators are called upon to serve inclusively, they run against both the exclusionary impulse of special education as well as the "normative center" (Florian, 2019) of general education. A figured identity that espouses an alternative identity of *inclusive* educator affords little to reduce the disconnect with their *positional* identities as special educators.

Teacher understandings of their competence are linked to the opportunities they have to practice their professional roles (Naraian, 2016). For example, if general educators are expected to take the lead on curriculum planning, they are more likely to see themselves as holding a higher status than their special education counterparts who, as we saw in many of our participants' experiences, are then often reduced to taking up assisting and tutoring roles in the classroom. We saw this, for example, with Jessica who constituted her teaching and enactments of inclusion from an ancillary position premised on her co-teacher's, students' and administrations' expectations for her as a special educator. Rena similarly had to work to figure out her own professional identity vis-a-vis her secondary positionings in the classroom. Such instances are symptomatic of the historical development of general education, whose reforms have remained largely impervious to developments within special education resulting in many "missed opportunities" for not only learning from each other, but for promoting greater inclusivity in our schools (Blanton, Pugach, & Boveda, 2018).

Such co-evolution (or the lack thereof) means that applications of notions of teacher competence for inclusion must make clearly visible the presumed relations between special and general education on which it is grounded. Teachers' enactments of inclusion index the messy entanglements of contradictory, ideas, roles, policies and practices that implicate the melding of these systems. Indeed, we suggest that the concept of *inclusion* itself must accommodate such entanglement in ways that reflect the relational contexts in which teacher competence is both recognized and realized. We may argue that just as inclusion is forged within such complexity, teachers' understanding of their competence too emerges from within the same. Teachers and "inclusion" are not ontologically separate entities; they do not come into being separately from each other; rather, they are jointly constituted. "Inclusion" cannot be understood solely as a concept or outcome *for* which we need to prepare teachers. To understand what "inclusion" means, we need to simultaneously understand how teachers make that happen.

The Material-Discursive Nature of Teachers' Agency for Inclusion

In our descriptions of our teacher-participants in this book, we deliberately selected theoretical frames that would permit us to address the material and discursive conditions within which teachers enacted their commitments to inclusion. In the following pages, we address the learnings we derived from that process and their significance for understanding inclusion.

The Affective Production of Teaching for Inclusion

An affective theoretical lens invites us to consider the embodied and emotional, the non-cognitive, the non-rational, forces that move and motivate us in our lives. Feelings of fear, shame, pain, happiness, and pleasure are all attached to particular objects and through our anticipation of such feelings we move towards or away from these objects (Ahmed, 2010). These affective attachments are felt in the body but are produced through social and cultural constructions and relationships (Blackman & Venn, 2010) becoming what Cvetcovich (2012) has described as a "public feeling" experienced within the individual. In the field of critical disability studies, affect theory can be seen as an entry point to "think about the ways in which affect economies draw

disabled people and those close to them into particular ways of feeling and emoting" (Goodley, Liddiard, & Runswick-Cole, 2018, p.206).
Scholars in this field have highlighted historical and contemporary
associations of disability with feelings of disgust, shame, fear, attrac-
tion, and fetishization (Hughes, 2012; Schweik, 2009) in explorations of
the "public feeling" towards disabled bodies. These affective attachments to disabled bodies and disability move people towards and away
from individuals with disabilities, figuratively and physically. These
may occur in the ways that non-disabled people interact with individuals with disabilities, or choose not to interact, as well as in the ways that
individuals with disabilities construct their own identities.

Alongside the affects that move through interactions with and about
disability, there are also affective attachments to success and failure in
education that move educators. Failure in school has been the rationale
for dismissal of students, teachers, and administrators. Students who
do not "meet schools' expectations for success" (Deschenes, Cuban,
& Tyack, 2001, p.527) have been labeled as everything from "lag-
gard," "depraved," "wayward," and "culturally deprived," to "learning disabled," "emotionally disturbed," "at risk," and "less fortunate."
Teachers are conceived of as failing when they are unable to remedi-
ate or fix perceived deficits in their students. Teacher failure is consequently inextricably linked to student failure. Fear of failure and desire
for success circulate and move teachers towards some "objects" and
away from others even before encountering said "objects" themselves
because the objects are already anticipated to cause dis/pleasure, dis/
comfort or dis/gust (Ahmed, 2014). Pedagogical acts are more than pedagogical acts. They are objects of fear or desire, and teachers are moved
towards or away from their enactment depending on their own histories, ideological positioning, cultural and structural contexts, and thus,
affective draws.

In our own work, we chose to take up an affective lens in part
because of our own commitments to complex understandings of teacher
becoming and the potential afforded by affect theory for understanding
teachers' attachments to inclusivity and its enactments in schooling.
This theoretical curiosity was substantiated by our participants as we

had known them as students and their experiences in their first year of teaching. This group of novice teachers was clearly committed to social justice as enacted through inclusive education and deeply engaged in the intellectual exploration of disability from a poststructuralist perspective (even if they did not all articulate it as such). Where other cohorts sometimes complained about "too much theory" or struggled to see the implications of theory for practice, these students asked for more theoretical analysis of their student teaching experiences. And yet, when they began teaching, they encountered the same, if not more, conflicts as other cohorts of students. If intellectually curious and personally committed students encountered similar struggles as those who had not embraced the usefulness of theory for informing their practice, a deeper analysis of their experiences was warranted in order to better understand our own work in educating teachers to teach inclusively. Affect theory, that recognizes the significance of the embodied experience on our individual trajectories of learning, growth and enactment, allowed us to explore more fully the forces that circulated with and through these teachers as they figured themselves as inclusive educators. As an analytic tool, it disclosed affective forces of success, goodness, smartness, and ability circulating in schools and the way these forces interacted with the teachers in this study to directly impact their enactments of inclusion.

In the experiences of the participants in this study, their enactments of inclusive pedagogy were mediated by their own perceptions of their competence. Those self-perceptions contribute to the "public feeling" (Cvetkovich, 2012) of successful teaching, or in this case, of successful inclusive teaching. For example, even as Harley could list and carry out the practices of teaching for inclusion, preconceived, socially constructed scripts around the role of special educator, professionalism, and femininity moved her through various relationships to the enactment of those practices. Feeling more or less able to enact specific practices with efficacy contributed to Harley's own sense of success as an inclusive educator, and consequently to the production of the idea of the "successful inclusive educator." For each participant, their individual context, inclusive of their own unique histories, encompassed affective forces that worked on and through them, moved them to action and inaction, contributed to their enactments of inclusion and to an understanding of themselves in relation to this constructed ideal. These feelings were many, varied, and *big*. In our own preparation of teachers to teach for inclusion, we have dedicated our efforts to helping teachers understand the epistemological underpinnings of systems of exclusion. We have focused on the theories that disrupt difference as sufficient for the enactment of inclusion, while attending less to embodied attachments to the very same notions of deviance, success, goodness, and failure that circulate around this phenomenon of difference, especially in schooling. Attending to the affective in this book has highlighted for us how significant those attachments are in teachers' *"becoming"* and their conceptions of self as successful, or even competent, inclusive educators. It confirms the need to prepare teachers for uncertain outcomes and also for us to embrace this ambiguity as a salient feature of inclusion.

Posthuman Approaches and the (De)Centering of Teachers

Attending to teachers' embodiment within the phenomenon of inclusion reflects an orientation to experience that does not privilege the mind but recognizes the role of the body within encounters with the world. This emphasis on "bodily processes and corporeal capacities" (Coole & Frost, 2010) is an important element within post-humanist approaches that eschew the Cartesian divide, that is, the privileging of mind over matter. Indeed, matter, within posthumanisms is not inert and passive but vibrant and agentive (Barad, 2007; Braidotti, 2018). In recent years, the "materialist" turn within the social sciences has produced increasing interest in post-humanist orientations to phenomena. Whereas humanism upholds a rational, self-conscious, autonomous individual, posthumanism challenges the status of the *human* (Nayar, 2014). It seeks to dismantle the boundaries between humans and other species, including plants, animals, machines, positing instead an entangled phenomenon that cannot be collapsed within a single, self-contained consciousness of the human. The "human" is a human-plant-animal-machine assemblage rather than an individuated organism that exists apart from other species. Increasingly, world-wide geological events have compelled scholars to challenge anthropocentricism—the sovereign status granted to the human species—in pursuit of deeper understanding of the cross-species entanglements that produce phenomena.

Our decision to explore post-humanist approaches in understanding the practice of our teachers derives from our empathy with the increasing restlessness among social science researchers with the over-reliance on discourse in the investigation of phenomena (Alaimo & Hekman, 2008). Like other scholars in this tradition, we sought to fold the material within our analyses in ways that did not posit a material-discursive binary. Additionally, we recognize that the humanist impulse itself draws on Enlightenment ideals that are premised on a white, rational, autonomous, male individual, which marginalizes individuals from historically marginalized communities, including disabled students and students of color (Plummer, 2011).

The de-centering of the human within a post-humanist stance clearly presents a challenge when inquiring into the work of inclusive educators. The rejection of an *ideology of ability* and the commitments to equity and justice that constitute the heart of an inclusive educator's foundation for practice are no longer available as the sole route to evaluating one's efficacy in doing this work. It does, however, allow us to recognize that the entanglement of the individual with other material and non-material entities cannot be addressed by merely a nod to the external context; rather, it attests to the becoming of the individual only in relation to other actors (human and non-human) whose roles are themselves unpredictable and changing. Teacher agency, we may understand, is a contingent phenomenon and always more-than-human. Yet, we have to ask: in light of continual affronts to the human rights of individuals all over the world, what ethical commitments can flow from such a post-humanist approach?

Some scholars who are unwilling to abandon humanism in an era marked by increasing social, political and economic inequalities, suggest the concept of a posthuman *human*. Such a position compels us, as researchers, to always consider materiality within our analyses. It recognizes that there may be a mismatch between our ideological attachments and the material conditions within which they are enacted. Therefore, it eschews certainty for an "epistemological modesty" that acknowledges the partial and situated nature of our pronouncements (Ellis, 2018). The categories and concepts that inform our commitments to inclusion must always be subject to scrutiny; "difference" is not a pre-given phenomenon but emerges contingently within the web of entanglements that constitutes inclusion in any setting. For teachers, a post-humanist response that continually engages with the materiality of their own experience as well as that of their students, allows them to understand their own development (alongside that of their students) as contingent while leaving open the possibility of creating new assemblages in which that can occur. For instance, by building a relationship with a family, they have already set in motion a new assemblage which may constitute a student's experience (and their own) with school. Or, when a teacher learns to use the particular assistive technology that can be utilized by a student, they have entered into a new assemblage with her. In other words, teachers are engaged in continually *becoming* with the world.

Goodley, Lawthon, and Runswick-Cole (2014) develop an alternative post-humanist approach that may be generative in other ways. Invoking the history of individuals with intellectual disabilities, they suggest that disability has always been *posthuman*. Humanist assumptions about a rational, autonomous subject have for long worked to confer *subhuman* status on disabled individuals. Yet, many of the same individuals have also had to work on both sides of the human/non-human binary. On the one hand, their experiences have provoked us to challenge humanist ideals of independence and individual agency, offering instead interdependence and relational agency as viable routes to achieving human dignity. On the other hand, they have to continually claim the capability to achieve the norms that can signal their *abilities* as humans. Goodley, Runswick-Cole, and Liddiard (2015) refer to this necessary maneuvering on both sides of the binary as reflecting a *dis*human position. They propose that disability brings a critical and political element to posthumanism, defining *dis*humanism as "the theoretical, political and practical work done to the category of the human by the presence of disability" (p. 6). A theory of *dis*humanism may inform all facets of experience where binaries operate—such as development, learning, school, family, etc.—to disclose the norms that underlies the expression of such experience while simultaneously seeking to trouble it. They identify such phenomena as Dis/medicine, Dis/youth, Dis/science, Dis/capitalism as sites where identities may be formed across binaries.

Even as *dis*humanism re-ignites the focus on equity that may easily be obscured within post-humanist studies, it may also be helpful in restoring to some degree the importance of personal narratives. Within a post-humanist turn where the individual is no longer the primary agent within phenomena and where multiple entities (human and non-human) are each understood as exercising agency, the epistemic value of narrative may be disputed. Yet, it is precisely the narratives of individuals with intellectual disabilities and their families upon which they draw, that surfaces the uniquely *posthuman* character of disability. In a similar vein, our own efforts to straddle a commitment to our participants as primary agents alongside analyses that situate them among other material-discursive "agents" surfaces the epistemic value of their experiences as necessary for any understanding of inclusion.

Following Goodley, Runswick-Cole, and Liggard (2015), we tentatively posit our experimental efforts in this book to lie in the realm of Dis/Narrative. If the hope of these authors for a *dis*human stance is that ultimately "thinking about the human will always involve thinking about disability" (p.6), then on a smaller scale, we might argue that Dis/Narrative is about both taking up conventional norms of narrative while simultaneously seeking to trouble the norms that govern them. In presenting the stories of Taiyo, Molly, Peter, Harley, Jessica, Adam, and Rena, we "centered" them by attending to the ways they made sense of their experiences and inviting them to add their reflections alongside us. We simultaneously "de-centered" them in some of our analyses by locating them within assemblages that constituted the phenomena they described to us. We could not have done the latter without the former. The appropriation of disability studies insights for understanding *teachers* (rather than students with disabilities) may trouble some readers. We suggest tentatively that this may be necessary if "inclusion" is not to be decoupled from (dis)ability. We continue to uphold the importance of teachers' stories for a complex understanding of inclusion, even as we register the growing recognition that solely humanist approaches may be insufficient in today's times to describe phenomena in complex ways.

Conclusion: The Necessity for Theorizing Practice for a Theory of Inclusion

The premise of this book has been that stories of teacher experiences are vital for deepening our understandings of inclusion. We follow Lytle and Cochran-Smith (1992) in recognizing the epistemic value of teacher practice for theorizing inclusion. Teacher practices toward inclusion can afford us new ways of continually refining what we mean by inclusion such that it remains responsive to the complex contexts in which it is enacted. Theorizing teacher practice allows us to also shift our understanding of teacher capacity for inclusion from a static property oriented towards abstract ideals, to a fluid and shifting engagement with competing material-discursive elements.

Acknowledging the material-discursive nature of teachers' enactments orients us differently to both inclusion and to teacher capacity for inclusive practice. We are compelled to consider inclusion as a material-discursive phenomenon and teachers' agency within such phenomenon may be understood as contextualized rather than an internal property. By "contexts" we mean all the different ways in which people, resources, ideas are continually moved, arranged and distributed across time and space. Such movement and arrangements are themselves reflective of local, national and global (re)configurations of the relations between teachers, schools and society. For example, neoliberal impulses that condition schooling through standardized measures of accountability equally inform the ways in which teachers are required to understand themselves as inclusive educators. Such accountability measures owe their character in no small part to global phenomena that include not only international comparisons of student learning and the increasing influence of privatization in schools and teacher preparation, but also rising nationalism and state-sanctioned discourses of "us" and "them" that pit students, teachers and communities against each other.

Working within and against these precarious conditions, we may think of teachers less as delivering heroic acts of resistance, and more as engaged in everyday negotiations that may themselves be characterized as "heroic" in the deliberate decision-making that is called for to reconcile competing priorities. Molly's decision to use a text her students could read and would engage with, Adam's calling of a #BlackLivesMatter assembly, or Taiyo's seamless integration of poetry and art into his curricula are self-conscious actions designed to accomplish a purpose not fostered within a neoliberal schooling agenda and in that regard, remain heroic.

We could propose, therefore, an understanding of inclusion as "a dynamic, open-ended arrangement of people, practices and ideas that are weighted, distributed and activated with uneven intensities across a system at any given point in time" (Naraian, 2018). Teachers are embedded within such systems and their work is entangled with the fluctuation and variability that characterizes them. The "change(s)" they are expected to enact as inclusive educators are intertwined with the multiple shifts and pulsations that are produced at various times and spaces. This means that rather than "agents of change" we need to see teachers as "changing agents" who both change and are changed by the contexts within which they enact their commitments. This need not mean that teacher agency for inclusion is always diminished. Acknowledging agency as contingent allows for the fact that teachers may continue to invest in growing their professional capacities so that they may enter into different assemblages within and outside their schools. Such new assemblages may stimulate new forms of inclusive practice that can in turn offer other conditions for exercising agency.

Note

1 Naraian & Schlessinger (2018).

References

Ahmed, S. (2010). *The promise of happiness*. Durham, NC: Duke University Press.

Ahmed, S. (2014). *Willful subjects*. Durham, NC: Duke University Press.

Alaimo, S., & Hekman, S. (Eds.) (2008). *Material feminisms*. Blooington, IND: Indiana University Press.

Barad, K. (2007). *Meeting the universe halfway: Quantum physics and the entanglement of matter and meaning*. Durham, NC: Duke University Press.

Blackman, L., & Venn, C. (Eds.) (2010). Special issue on affect: Editorial. *Body & Society, 16* (1), 7–28.

Blanton, L. P., Pugach, M. C., & Boveda, M. (2018). Interrogating the intersections between general and special education in the history of teacher education reform. *Journal of Teacher Education, 69*(4), 354–366.

Booth, T., & Ainscow, M. (2002). *Index for inclusion: Developing learning and participation in schools*. Centre for Studies on Inclusive Education (CSIE). England: Bristol BS16 1QU.

Braidotti, R. (2018). A theoretical framework for the critical posthumanities. *Theory, Culture and Society*, 1–31. Special issue.

Clandinin, D. J., & Connelly, M. F. (1996). Teachers' professional knowledge landscapes: Teacher stories. Stories of teachers. School stories. Stories of schools. *Educational Researcher, 25*(3), 24–30.

Clandinin, D. J., & Connelly, F. M. (2000). *Narrative inquiry: Experience and story in qualitative research*. San Francisco, CA: Joey Bass.

Coole, D., & Frost, S. (Eds.) (2010). Introducing the new materialisms. In *New materialisms: Ontology, agency and politics*. Durham, NC: Duke University Press.

Cvetkovich, A. (2012). *Depression: A public feeling*. Durham, NC: Duke University Press.

Danforth, S., & Naraian, S. (2015). This new field of inclusive education: Beginning a dialogue on conceptual foundations. *Intellectual and Developmental Disabilities, 53*(1), 70–85.

Danielson, C. (2016). Charlotte Danielson on rethinking teacher evaluation. *Education Week, 35*(28), 20-24.

Deschenes, S., Cuban, L., & Tyack, D. (2001). Mismatch: Historical perspectives on schools and students who don't fit them. *Teachers College Record, 103*(4), 525–547.

Ellingson, L. L. (2011). Analysis and representation across the continuum. In N. K. Denzin & Y. S. lincoln (Eds.), *The Sage handbook of qualitative research* (pp. 595–610). Thousand Oaks, CA: Sage.

Ellis, C. (2018). *Antebellum posthuman: Race and materiality in the mid-nineteenth century*. New York: Fordham University.

Florian, L. (2019). On the necessary co-existence of special and inclusive education. *International Journal of Inclusive Education, 23*(7–8), 691–704.

Goodley, D., Lawthom, R., & Runswick Cole, K. (2014). Posthuman disability studies. *Subjectivity, 7*(4), 342–361.

Goodley, D., Runswick-Cole, K., & Liddiard, K. (2015). The DisHuman child. *Discourse: Studies in the cultural politics of education. 37*(5), 770-784.

Goodley, D., Runswick-Cole, K., & Liddiard, K. (2018). Feeling disability: Theories of affect and critical disability studies. *Disability & Society, 33*(2), 197–217.

Graham, L. J., & Slee, R. (2008). An illusory interiority: Interrogating the discourse/s of inclusion. *Educational Philosophy and Theory, 40*(2), 277–293.

Holland, D., Lachiotte, Jr., W., Skinner, D., & Cain, C. (1998). *Identity and agency in cultural worlds.* Cambridge, MA: Harvard University Press.

Hughes, B. (2012). Fear, pity and disgust: Emotions and the non-disabled imaginary. In N. Watson, A. Roulstone & C. Thomas (Eds.), *Handbook of disability* (pp.67–78). London: Routledge.

Huntly, H. (2008). Teachers' work: Beginning teachers' conceptions of competence. *The Australian Educational Researcher, 35*(1), 125–145.

Lytle, S., & Cochran-Smith, M. (1992). Teacher research as a way of knowing. *Harvard Educational Review, 62*(4), 447–475.

Naraian, S. (2016). Spatializing student learning to re-imagine the "place" of inclusion. *Teachers College Record, 118*(12), 1–46.

Naraian, S. (2018). Teaching for inclusion. *International Conference on the Evolution towards an Inclusive Education System.* UNIA, The Interfederal Centre for Equal Opportunities and Opposition to Racism, Brussels, Belgium, October 8–9, 2018.

Naraian, S. (2019). Precarious, debilitated, ordinary: Rethinking (in)capacity for inclusion. *Curriculum Inquiry, 49*(4), 464–484.

Naraian, S., & Schlessinger, S. (2018). Becoming an inclusive educator: Agentive maneuverings in collaboratively taught classrooms. *Teaching and Teacher Education, 71,* 179–189.

Nayar, P. K. (2014). *Posthumanism.* Malden, MA: Polity Press.

Plummer, K. (2011). Critical humanism and queer theory: Living with the tensions. In N. K. Denzin & Y. S. Lincoln (Eds.), *The SAGE handbook of qualitative research* (pp. 195–207). Thousand Oaks, CA: Sage.

Schweik, S. (2009). *The ugly laws: Disability in public.* New York: New York University Press.

Slee, R. (2011). *The irregular school: Exclusion, schooling and inclusive education.* Milton Park, Abingdon, Oxfordshire: Routledge.

Stevens, D. (2010). A Freirean critique of the competence model of teacher education, focusing on the standards for qualified teacher status in England. *Journal of Education for Teaching, 36*(2), 187–196.

Stillman, J. (2011). Teacher learning in an era of high-stakes accountability: Productive tension and critical professional practice. *Teachers College Record, 113*(1), 133–180.

Index

Disability Studies in Education

GENERAL EDITORS: SUSAN L. GABEL & SCOT DANFORTH

The book series Disability Studies in Education is dedicated to the publication of monographs and edited volumes that integrate the perspectives, methods, and theories of disability studies with the study of issues and problems of education. The series features books that further define, elaborate upon, and extend knowledge in the field of disability studies in education. Special emphasis is given to work that poses solutions to important problems facing contemporary educational theory, policy, and practice.

To order other books in this series, please contact our Customer Service Department:

peterlang@presswarehouse.com (within the U.S.)
orders@peterlang.com (outside the U.S.)

Or browse by series:

WWW.PETERLANG.COM